John Britton, Thomas Rees

Reminiscences of Literary London from 1779-1853.

With Interesting Anecdotes of Publishers, Authors and Book Auctioneers of that

Period, &c., &c

John Britton, Thomas Rees

Reminiscences of Literary London from 1779-1853.
With Interesting Anecdotes of Publishers, Authors and Book Auctioneers of that Period, &c., &c

ISBN/EAN: 9783337280888

Printed in Europe, USA, Canada, Australia, Japan

Cover: Foto ©Thomas Meinert / pixelio.de

More available books at **www.hansebooks.com**

Reminiscences

OF

Literary London

From 1779 to 1853.

With Interesting Anecdotes of Publishers,
Authors and Book Auctioneers
of that Period, &c., &c.

BY

Dr. THOMAS REES,

WITH EXTENSIVE ADDITIONS BY

JOHN BRITTON, F. S. A.

Edited by a Book Lover.

NEW YORK:
FRANCIS P. HARPER.
1896.

THESE interesting "Literary Reminiscences," written about 1853, and privately issued, are known to but few persons, as but a limited number of copies were printed for presentation. The volume includes extensive recollections of Authors, Publishers, and Booksellers from 1779 to 1853. The authors were personally acquainted with all the prominent writers, artists, and makers of books, and many curious anecdotes, prices received by authors for their well-known works, editions sold, and personal peculiarities of literary and business men here given will be new to the reader. The work is now for the first time edited, with the hope that it may prove as enjoyable reading to the purchaser as it has been to the

New York, 1896.   *BOOK LOVER.*

PREFACE

By John Britton.

ST. PAUL'S Churchyard, Ave-Maria Lane and Amen Corner were familiar names to the eye and mind in my boy-days; but I had no more notion of the features and character of the places than of the interior of a man-of-war, or of Robinson Crusoe's island. After reading numerous magazines, and taking in several of the sixpenny numbers published by Harrison, Cooke, Parsons, etc., and thereby ascertaining something about authors, artists, printers, and booksellers, I became curious and anxious to see such gifted personages, their homes, or haunts; and also where the manufacturers of literature resided, what were their peculiarities, and who and what sort of beings they were. I also coveted to see and read more books than I could afford to purchase. During the apprenticeship, I do not remember to have had an opportunity of satisfying this curiosity, except early in a morning, before shops were opened, or on Sundays, when they were all closed, and "The Row," with its appendages, as

PREFACE.

dull and silent as many village churchyards; but after being relieved from my apprentice-bondage, I found my way to the famed book-mart; traversed the narrow, dark street, miscalled Row; stopped to gaze at every shop window, and even stealthily looked in at every opened doorway, to see if a Harrison, a Cooke, a Hogg, or even one of their Grub-street workmen, or a rich author, could be descried. The names of Peter Pindar, Thomas Holcroft, Dr. Buchan, Wm. Godwin, Dr. A. Rees, Mr. Howard, Mr. Hall, Thos. Paine, the Misses Porter, Hannah More, Mrs. Radcliffe, and many others were familiar to me, and I longed to see such super-human beings, as I then regarded them. At length I ventured to enter some of the houses, and thus obtain a sight of labelled numbers, and volumes of new publications, and also the persons and faces of some of their proprietors. At that time most of the tradesmen attended in their respective shops, and dwelt in the upper parts of their houses; now, the heads of many of the large establishments visit their counting-houses only for a few hours in the day, and leave the working part to junior partners, clerks, and apprentices. Vast and numerous changes have taken place in the publishing and bookselling business since I first haunted Paternoster Row, and book-stalls; and many and important improvements have been introduced into all the essentials of book-making. Paper, type, ink, compositorship, and press-work, have advanced from almost the lowest to nearly the highest degree of perfection. The number and qualifications of authors have progressed in nearly an equal ratio. This assertion, I believe, will be fully verified, by referring to, and comparing, the books and periodicals which were published at the end of the last century with those of the year 1852. It would not be a difficult task to exemplify this by explaining the varieties and dissimilarities between the material and mental characteristics of literature of the two epochs; but I must limit myself to a brief account of Paternoster Row.

This far-famed thoroughfare is commonly said to derive its name from the stationers, or text-writers, who formerly dwelt there, and dealt mostly in religious books, horn-books, and others, which were marketable before the Reformation. It more probably had its appellation from the rosary, or pater-noster makers, a more thriving trade than bookselling, before Henry the Eighth, of revolutionary memory, commanded the books of Luther to be burnt in the Churchyard.

Strype, in his edition of Stow's "Survey of Lon-

PREFACE.

don," 1720, says, "This street, before the fire of London (1666), was taken up by eminent mercers, silkmen, and lacemen; and their shops were so resorted to by the nobility and gentry, in their coaches, that oft-times the street was so stopped up that there was no room for foot passengers." Soon after that conflagration most of these moved to the vicinity of Covent Garden. Some of the mercers and silkmen renewed their residences in this spot in new houses; but near the east end there were "stationers and large warehouses for booksellers; well situated for learned and studious men's access thither, being more retired and private." St. Paul's Churchyard appears to have been the chief mart of the bookselling trade at the time of the great fire. Dugdale told Pepys that more than £150,000 worth of books were destroyed on that fatal occasion. Previous to this epoch, Little Britain, and Duke Street adjoining, seem to have been the most noted site for booksellers.

However sanguine my young imagination may have been, I did not dare to anticipate the possibility of ever writing or publishing a book; still less of being on friendly terms with the many partners of the largest publishing establishment in the world. Yet such has been my lot; and having indulged the habit of continually visiting Paternoster Row, on the last day of every month for more than forty years, it has become identified with many and various associations and connexions of deep and exciting interest; and I have often meditated on writing an account of this literary emporium. But I have thought it advisable to solicit my old and esteemed friend, Dr. Thomas Rees, to indulge me with his opinions and recollections on this subject. With his usual kindness and courtesy he promptly favoured me with the following letter, to which I have subjoined a few memoranda of my own.

My Dear Britton,

You ask me to furnish some reminiscences of Paternoster Row, in the earlier period of my acquaintance with it, towards the conclusion of the last, and the commencement of the present, century. Our long and intimate connection, our kindred pursuits, and our joint labours on some occasions, in the same field of literary research, render it difficult for me to meet your wishes with a denial; at the same time I feel very sensibly that in recurring to a period so long past, between which and the present, half a century has intervened, important matters relating both to events and persons may have escaped my recollec-

PREFACE.

tion, or may be recalled too indistinctly and imperfectly to be of real value for a practical object. I will, however, endeavour to revive the image of this locality, as it appeared to my view at the period alluded to; and to awaken the memory of such facts and incidents relating to the character and enterprises of its inhabitants, as may be likely to afford some interest or amusement to your readers.

DR. THOMAS REES.

Contents.

PART I.

Paternoster Row, Past and Present, and its Booksellers—Harrison's Publications—Dr. Busby—Charles Cooke—Alexander Hogg—The Rivingtons—Booksellers' Signs—Annual Register—London Magazine—The Baldwins—The Robinsons—J. Scott—Alexander Chalmers and his Publications—The Longmans—Owen Rees—Thomas Hurst—Chambers' and Rees' Cyclopædia—Annual Review—W. Taylor and R. Southey—Authors and their Publishers—Lardner's Cyclopædia—Third Class of Booksellers—Trade Auctioneers—Peter Pindar—Rees' Cyclopædia—P. Courtier—Miss Mitford—W. Pinnock—Ave Maria Lane—Whittaker's—H. G. Bohn—Stationers' Court—Stationers' Hall—St. Paul's Churchyard—Francis Newberry—Joseph Johnson—Sir Richard Phillips—C. Bowles—J. Mawman—Thomas Hood.......pages 19 to 87

PART II.

Fleet Street and its Immediate Vicinity—McCreery—Nightingale Rylance—John Major—Walton and Cotton's Angler—Walpole Anecdotes—Rev. T. F. Dibdin—Kearsley—Quarterly Review—John Murray—George Cruikshank—W. Hone and his Trials—Wm. Cobbett—E. Williams—The John Bull—London Magazine and its Contributors—J. Taylor—J. H. Wiffin—Duke of Bedford—T. Bensley—Red Lion Passage—John Nichols and his Literary Anecdotes—A. J. Valpy—Wm. Pickering—The Bridgewater Treatises—High Holborn—The Architectural Antiquities of Great Britain—John Britton's Partners—O. Rees—Josiah Taylor..............................pages 89 to 126

PART III.

The Strand at the beginning of the Century—Thomas Caddell—The Newspaper Press—George Lane—D. Stuart—John Bell—Rudolph Ackermann and his publications—F. Shoberl, Author and Editor—Annuals—"Dr. Syntax"—Combe—Rowlandson—John and Leigh Hunt—The Literary Gazette—Richardson's Auctions—Geographers—Prince Sanders — Lyceum Theatre—Auctioneers—The Sothebys—Evans—The Christies' Sale-Rooms—Pall Mall—King Street—Covent Garden—Hogarth's Election — P. Luckombe—King and Lochee's Auction Rooms; their book-sales.............................pages 127 to 174

Part I.

PATERNOSTER ROW

AND ITS VICINITY.

Part I.

PATERNOSTER ROW
AND ITS VICINITY.

Paternoster Row, Past and Present, and its Booksellers—Harrison's Publications— Dr. Busby—Charles Cooke—Alexander Hogg—The Rivingtons—Booksellers' Signs—Annual Register—London Magazine—The Baldwins—The Robinsons—J. Scott—Alexander Chalmers and his Publications—The Longmans—Owen Rees—Thomas Hurst—Chambers' and Rees' Cyclopædia—Annual Review—W. Taylor and R. Southey—Authors and their Publishers—Lardner's Cyclopædia—Third Class of Booksellers—Trade Auctioneers—Peter Pindar—Rees' Cyclopædia—P. Courtier— Miss Mitford –W. Pinnock—Ave Maria Lane—Whittaker's—H. G. Bohn—Stationers' Court—Stationers' Hall—St. Paul Churchyard— Francis Newberry—Joseph Johnson—Sir Richard Phillips—C. Bowles—J. Mawman—Thomas Hood.

NEAR the close of the eighteenth century, "The Row," as it is now popularly called, contained two or more printing establishments, one of which was conducted by the late "George Woodfall," who had succeeded his father, Henry Sampson Woodfall, well known as the printer and publisher of the "Public Advertiser," in which appeared the far-famed "Letters of Junius." The latter was still living, and I had the pleasure of seeing him in the enjoyment of a "green old age," when I first visited London. Those daring epistles, with the newspaper in which they were published, excited intense curiosity during the course of their publication. There were also two houses of wholesale stationers; one belonging to the family of Key, and the other to Peter Wynn. The University of Oxford had, under the management of Mr. Gardner, a depot to supply the London trade with their editions of Bibles and Prayer-books. But with these, and a few other exceptions, the majority of the houses were tenanted by persons who were strictly, in the ordinary sense, Booksellers. The varieties of these may be classed under three divisions. The first comprehends publishers only, whose sale of books was confined to their own property. The second might be designated book-merchants, who were chiefly wholesale dealers, and carried on an extensive and important trade with country booksellers; they were also publishers upon a large scale, both of periodicals, under the designation of magazines, and reviews; and likewise works on general literature and science, of the larger and more important and costly descriptions. The third were chiefly retail traders, mostly in old books, but in some instances were publishers of pamphlets, and books of comparatively small expense.

In the first class, at the time under consideration, three persons were conspicuous, viz.: Harrison, Cooke, and Hogg. The first, on many accounts, is entitled to pre-eminence, as he took the lead in a class of publications which deserve great praise for valuable improvements in their editorial qualities, and particularly in pictorial illustrations.

It is not easy to pronounce decidedly the exact time when books of magnitude were first divided into small portions and issued periodically in numbers; but Harrison may be said to be one of the first persons who embarked, with much spirit and upon an extensive scale, in such a mode of publication. His first speculation of the sort was "The Novelist's Magazine," which embraced several of the larger standard and popular English novels then known. They were printed in octavo, in double columns, stitched up in small numbers, and published weekly, at sixpence each. The most striking feature of this publication, and one of its chief attractions, consisted of engraved embellishments. Harrison had the judgment to select artists of acknowledged merit, who afterwards rose to distinguished eminence; including Stothard, R. Corbould, Smirke, and Burney; whilst the engravings bear the names of Heath, Sharpe, Grignion, Smith, Milton, Neagle, etc. The "Novelist's Magazine," commenced by him in 1779, extended to twenty-three good-sized volumes. Its popularity may be estimated by the fact that, at one time 12,000 copies of each number were sold, weekly. The success of this work encouraged Harrison to publish, on the same plan, with embellishments by the same eminent artists, "The New Novelist's Magazine," a series of short tales; which was followed by "The British Classics," embracing the Spectator, Tatler, Guardian, Connoisseur, etc., of which a very large edition was sold. These publications still maintain their credit; and clean copies, with good impressions of the plates, are puchased at fair prices. He also produced a corresponding work, entitled "The Sacred Classics."

The same publisher embarked in another literary speculation, somewhat singular in its plan; a "General Geography," upon a large scale, extending to forty numbers, in quarto, closely printed. He engaged to supply its purchasers, without additional charge, with a pair of twelve-inch globes. Harrison published "The British Magazine," in 3 vols., with beautiful engravings of portraits, views, and prints of historical and fancy subjects. These included also a large portion of Biographical, Historical, and Critical Essays, with Poetry. His next publication was "The Musical Magazine," which, in an octavo size, gave a selection of the works of the most eminent and popular composers, arranged for the piano-forte. The purchaser of the entire work was entitled to receive a square piano-forte. Dr. Busby, at that time a popular musical professor, was employed as editor, and the instruments were examined and attested by him. This gentleman was much employed by Sir Richard Phillips, in writing for the "Monthly Magazine," etc., and later in life made himself very conspicuous, and amenable to severe public criticism, by translating "Lucretius," and "giving living recitations of the translation, with tea and bread and butter," at his house in Queen Anne Street, to select parties of friends, who were invited to endure the one and relish the other. I was among the number, and must own that the display of poetry, oratory, and coxcombry was lamentably ludicrous. Never did I behold a young man more vain, impudent, and heartless, than the juvenile Busby, and rarely, perhaps, has the diploma of "Mus. Doc." appeared more ridiculous and degraded than by the conduct and appearances of the musical professor with his finical son. These gentlemen made a finishing exhibition of themselves on the re-opening of the famed Drury Lane Theatre, after its memorable rebuilding. It is very generally known that an Address was sought for amongst the authors of the age, and that in the mass presented was one from Lord Byron, accepted, and another from Dr. Busby rejected. The mortified and vain Doctor fancied that he could bring the committee to shame, if not repentance, by publishing his own poetry and prose, in a truly novel manner. Accordingly, he and his accomplished son were seen in the stage box of the theatre soon after its opening. At the end of the play the young gentleman leaped upon the stage, with his father's rejected address in one hand, and an opera hat in the other, and repeated the following lines:

> "When energizing objects men pursue,
> What are the miracles they cannot do?"

Here, however, the juvenile spouter was stopped by Mr. Raymond, the stage manager, and a constable, who handed the young gentleman off the stage. The "Rejected Addresses," by James and Horace Smith, contain a good burlesque imitation of the Busby address.

Amongst the periodicals of Harrison was "The Wit's Magazine," edited by Thos. Holcroft, and containing a variety of amusing articles both in prose and verse, written by the editor, by Mr. Harrison, and by other authors of talent. It was embellished with large prints, folded. His "Biographical Magazine,'" an 8vo. volume, contains small engraved portraits, with short notices of each subject, well executed.

Harrison issued two periodicals of smaller size, the "Pocket Magazine" and the "Lady's Pocket Magazine," which were published monthly, and embellished with portraits and a series of small engraved views of places, from drawings by the late J. M. W. Turner, R.A., who eventually became the most eminent landscape painter in the world. These works contained writings of several young authors, some of whom afterwards attained eminence; amongst them were my esteemed friends, the Misses Porter, and their brother, the poet, artist, and traveler. A frequent writer in these magazines was R. A. Davenport, who sometimes officiated as editor. Both Charles and Thomas Dibdin contributed many well-written and amusing papers; as did also Peter Courtier.

Contemporary with, and a near neighbour to

Harrison, was John Cooke, who for many years carried on a large and successful business as publisher of periodical works. He was probably one of the earliest of the Paternoster Row booksellers who applied himself to this branch of trade, upon a large scale. The subjects and form of his books and their illustrations were, however, very different from those of Harrison. Cooke confined himself, for some time, to religious publications, the principal and most popular of which was Southwell's "Commentary of the Bible;" it had a large sale, and produced a profit of many thousand pounds. After the appearance, in numbers, of Chambers' "Cyclopædia," under the editorial care of Dr. Abraham Rees, Cooke published an imitation, with the name of Hall, as editor, of some merit, but inferior to its predecessor. All Cooke's publications were in folio, divided into small portions, and issued weekly, at sixpence each number; they were "adorned with cuts," which were of the old school, both as to drawings and engravings.

At an advanced age Mr. Cooke retired to the country, with a handsome fortune, and died, in 1810, at the age of 79. His son, Charles, continued for some time his father's principal publications; but he soon commenced a new course, which was attended with great success. The copyright of Hume's "History of England," belonging to Cadell and Longman, having expired, Cooke availed himself of the circumstance to publish an edition, with Smollett's Continuation, in weekly numbers, at sixpence each. It was neatly printed, and embellished with portraits and vignettes tolerably executed. Contemporaneously with this, he also published a series of the older popular English Novels, with attractive embellishments. The original drawings and paintings, from which the prints were taken, were exhibited in a picture gallery, at the rear of his shop. At a later time Cooke published an edition of Bell's "British Theatre," under the editorship of Richard Cumberland. Besides inheriting a handsome fortune from his father, he acquired a considerable increase by his own speculations. He built a new house in Epping Forest, where he lived a short time, and died, in the prime of life, after a painful operation performed by Sir Astley Cooper. Although my (Britton) finances would not allow me to purchase the whole of Harrison's and Cooke's publications, I bought some of them, at what is technically called "trade price," and must own that they not only afforded me much amusement and instruction, on repeated perusal and examination, but, I believe, created that love of literature and art which progressively rose to a confirmed passion. The periodicals, by the publishers above noticed, were sought for and hailed with intense curiosity as they made their appearance; and I may safely aver that the embellished works, which I have since produced, sprang from the seeds which the Cookes and Harrisons sowed, at the end of the last century. The very beautiful and effective drawings and engravings by Stothard and Heath were eminently calculated to fascinate the young eye, as they gratified also that of the learned professor of art. Harrison's "British Magazine," of which three volumes were published in 1782, 3 and 4, contained several very highly-finished plates by Heath, from Stothard's designs. A short time before his decease I spent a day with Charles Cooke, at his rural villa, which had attained the cognomen of Cooke's Folly. Though expensively fitted up and furnished, it was wholly devoid of the elegancies of high life, and exhibited more ostentatious finery and show than classical or simple beauty. Its walls were, however, amply covered with paintings, drawings, and prints.

Alexander Hogg, who lived next door to Cooke, formed his literary schemes on the model of his neighbour. His publications were chiefly religious, and issued in weekly sixpenny numbers. The principal were, a "Bible with Annotations," by the Rev. Timothy Priestly, the brother of the eminent philosopher of that name. Like Cooke, Hogg brought out an "Encyclopædia," with the name of Howard, as editor. All his publications were in folio; with a profusion of most wretched prints. Miserable as these works were, both as to literary and artistic execution, their proprietor contrived to derive from them a handsome fortune. Amongst the books published by Hogg, was a large folio volume, called "Antiquities of England and Wales," with the name of Henry Boswell, as author, or editor. It has a great number of prints wofully executed, both as to drawing and engraving, and copied from any and every source that was accessible. For pirating one or more from Grose's "Antiquities," the publisher was sued, and sentenced to pay damages, with costs. The letter-press was quite in harmony with the prints, and equally valueless, being taken from any book or books that could be obtained, without acknowledgment. The editor is said to have been a servant of Hogg's, who was paid by the week for his services, in cutting up books for the printer, and reading the proofs.

That there was not much congeniality of sentiment, or friendly feeling between Harrison and Hogg, may be inferred by an epigram which the former wrote for and inserted in the "Lady's Pocket Magazine," July, 1795.

ON A STUPID BOOKSELLER.

By Peter Pindar Esq. (James Harrison.)

Thou Beast! amid the sons of Wisdom plac'd,
Who, times of old, as well as modern, grac'd,
Couldst thou not catch a portion of their fire?
Rolls not thine eye upon their works each day,
And canst thou, from them, nothing bear away,
To lift thy HOG-like soul above the mire?

At the period under consideration, Hogg's publishing business was conducted by a young man, familiarly known in the trade by the name of "Thomas," who was much liked by the booksellers' collectors. He served his master many years, and was with him when the latter died. He declined to serve in the same capacity under the son, who had previously been a stranger to the business; and therefore, after some demur, was admitted by the latter into partnership. The union did not last long. Hogg retired, and the business devolved on "Thomas," who introduced important changes into it, by which he raised the character of the house and improved his own fortune. He rose gradually in the esteem of his neighbours, and the shopman of Mr. Hogg is now deservedly respected as Mr. Alderman Thomas Kelly.

My next class comprises the greater wholesale booksellers and publishers, inhabitants of the Row. The first of these, at the sign of the "Bible and Crown," were the Rivingtons. Almost all the booksellers' houses of London, as well as those of other trades, were formerly contra-distinguished from each other by Signs, either over the doors, or projecting into the streets. The latter becoming a nuisance were prohibited by Act of Parliament; but the former are still continued, in many places. The following are some of those Signs: Bible and Ball; Anchor; Black Swan; Black Boy; Golden Anchor; Cicero's Head; Shakspere's Head; Red Lion; Ship and Black Swan; Raven; Sun; Bible and Crown; the Dunciad; and the Star.

The Rivingtons constitute an old and highly-respectable firm, with premises extending from the front to St. Paul's Churchyard. The earliest of this family whom I have been able to trace was Charles, whose name appears in the beginning of the eighteenth century. It is certain he carried on business here as early as 1710. In 1730 his name is joined with that of Thomas Longman and some others, as publishers of Thuanus's great historical work. He died in 1742, and was succeeded by his son, John. This family has always been distinguished for its zealous attachment to the Church of England, and has consequently enjoyed an intimate connexion with the established clergy. It is related of John Rivington, that he was a very assiduous attendant on the services in St. Paul's Church, and was seldom absent from the early morning prayers, at six or seven o'clock. If surprised by the bell before he had quitted his bed, he has been known to put on his clothes hastily, and finish dressing in the church, during the service. He died in 1792, at the age of 73, and was succeeded by his two sons, Francis and Charles, who constituted the firm when I first became acquainted with the Metropolis. The first died in 1822, and the second some time in 1831. The Rivingtons engaged largely in the publishing trade, but chiefly in books relating to the Established Church. In 1791, during the political and religious excitement produced by the French Revolution, they commenced the "British Critic," a monthly review of literature, professedly intended to uphold the tenets of the

Established Church, and the Tory politics of the ruling government. The principal and most influential periodical of this class was the "Monthly Review," which was ably conducted by Dr. Griffiths, who had the assistance of several eminent writers. The first number was published in May, 1749, when he carried on the trade of a bookseller at the "Dunciad," in Ludgate Street. In 1754 he removed to a new shop in Paternoster Row, afterwards occupied by H. D. Symonds, and in 1759 to the Strand, where he continued his original sign of the Dunciad. On relinquishing business in 1764, he committed the publication of the Review to Mr. Becket. Dr. Griffiths died at Turnham Green, in 1803. After his death the Review was conducted by his son, Colonel Griffiths. At his decease the copyright was sold, but the publication was not long continued. At the time of which I am writing, there were two other reviews, published monthly—the "Critical" and "Analytical"—both of which, as well as the "Monthly," were the property of the liberal dissenters. Under these circumstances it was thought desirable to bring out another Review, which should counteract and neutralize their principles as much as possible; and, at the same time, develop and sustain the religious and political opinions of the party who were attached to the Established Church. Hence originated the "British Critic," as an antagonistic publication. It was projected and conducted by two learned and able clergymen, the Rev. Richard Nares, and the Rev. Wm. Beloe, the translator of Herodotus, who were aided and supported in the undertaking by Dr. Parr and other eminent writers. It may well be supposed the articles contributed by such men were distinguished by erudition and general literary merits; and yet the Review was never, I believe, a popular or profitable work. Of late years it has been changed from a monthly to a quarterly publication. In association with Mr. Nares, was my old and much-respected friend, the Rev. John Whitaker, author of a Life of Mary, Queen of Scots, and of many other learned and "partycoloured" works. He was very severe in his criticisms on those authors whose religious and political opinions differed from his own prejudices.

Another periodical, published by the Rivingtons, was the Annual Register, originally brought out by Dodsley, with the literary aid of Edmund Burke. The Rivingtons purchased the copyright, and continued the work on its original Tory principles. It was for some years edited by Mr. R. A. Davenport. The principal books of the ornamental class published by the Rivingtons were those written by the late Mr. Donovan, on several subjects of natural history. He was an excellent naturalist, and an accurate and skillful draughtsman.

On the south side of the Row, near the premises described, was located Robert Baldwin, at the time of which I am writing. He was greatly esteemed as an upright and honourable tradesman. For many years he published the "London Magazine," which commenced almost as early as the "Gentleman's," the first number bearing the date of 1732. This was for many years a very popular periodical. Mr. Baldwin died in 1810. His nephew and successor commenced a new magazine in 1820, with the same title, under the avowed editorship of John Scott, a young author of excellent character and considerable literary talents. The work was proceeding very satisfactorily, and rising into popularity, when the editor was unhappily involved in a quarrel, which ended in a duel. The meeting was conducted by young men wholly unaccustomed to such affairs of "honour," and the fatal result of the rashness and inexperience of his second was the cause of the death of Mr. Scott. In traversing Lincolnshire for the Beauties of England, in the year 1810, I met Mr.

Scott, at Stamford, where he was engaged by Mr. Drakard, to edit a new weekly newspaper, which the latter had started. The high tone of politics and powerful writing of Mr. Scott soon attracted popularity, and the writer was invited to contribute articles to some of the London periodicals. These also excited both the admiration and envy of many readers and authors. A controversy arose in the London Magazine and in Blackwood's Edinburgh, which became sarcastic, vindictive, and personal, and ended as above stated, in a manner which created a mingled sensation of sorrow and horror in many minds. The magazines and newspapers of the time were much occupied, afterwards, with a succession of papers on the ceremonies, folly, and unhallowed practices of duelling. At the time of penning this note (June, 1852) "an affair of honour," as a duel is misnamed, has occurred between two "honourable gentlemen" of the House of Commons, which has fortunately turned the event into ridicule, and will be likely to produce good moral effects.

Charles Baldwin, brother of Robert, had an extensive printing business in Bridge Street, Blackfriars, and realized much profit by printing the "St. James's Chronicle," a newspaper which at one time attained great popularity. It is still conducted by his son, Charles, who is also its printer, and it is said he is joint proprietor of the "Morning Herald," and the "Standard." He is a gentleman of the highest respectability, and of extensive knowledge.

The Robinsons, at the end of the eighteenth and beginning of the nineteenth centuries, when I first became acquainted with the firm, carried on the largest business of any house in London, as general publishers, and also as wholesale and retail booksellers. George, the head and founder of the house, had been an assistant to John Rivington, and about 1763 embarked in business in partnership with John Robinson, at whose death, in 1776, he was left alone in the concern. His rising reputation for personal integrity and steady habits of business recommended him to the friendly notice of Thomas Longman, the second publisher of that name, who, well knowing the difficulties which young tradesmen had to encounter with a deficient capital, voluntarily offered to give him any credit he might require for books of his publication. By unremitting attention, and the judicious application of strong natural talents, his business steadily and rapidly increased, so that by the year 1780 his wholesale trade had become the largest in London. About that time, the necessity for assistants in the management of the concern led him to take into partnership his son, George, also the two brothers, John and James, the firm being then designated that of G., G., J. and J. Robinson. They published largely books of considerable size and of great value. The head of the firm was considered to have an excellent judgment in the difficult and often critical undertaking of the superintendence and management of the literary concerns of a publishing establishment. He greatly respected meritorious authors, and acted with singular liberality in his pecuniary dealings with them. Besides the works of which they were the sole proprietors, they were engaged jointly with several of the principal houses in numerous works of great extent, such as Kippis's "Biographia Britannica."

In 1780 they commenced the "Annual Register," following the plan of Dodsley's, but advocating a different system of politics. They engaged in the preparation and conducting of this work gentlemen of high character and established literary reputation, by which it soon acquired great popularity. The current sale of each volume, for many years, exceeded 7000 copies. They were also the publishers of the "Town and Country Magazine," of which there were sold about 14,000 copies, monthly; and of the "Ladies' Magazine," a publication for a long period of equal popularity and emolument. For many years the confidential friend and literary adviser of the house was the late Alexander Chalmers, who possessed many qualifications for that delicate and difficult office. He is said to have contributed largely to their several periodicals, and had a prominent share in the editorial direction of the "Biographical Dictionary," which extended to 32 volumes 8vo., and was in progress of publication from 1812 to 1817. Having often had occasion to refer to this work, in the expectation of finding full and accurate information, with discriminating comments on the writings and merits of the authors, whose memoirs it professes to narrate, I have too often been disappointed and mortified. A good Biographia Britannica is a literary desideratum. I cannot conscientiously praise the execution of this Dictionary, yet I feel sincere respect for the man, and admiration of many of his literary works. He was a truly estimable professional literary character, and it is said that "no man conducted so many works for the booksellers of London; and his attention to accuracy of collation; his depth and research as to facts, and his discrimination as to the character of the authors under his review, cannot be too highly praised." Such is the remark of Mr. Timperley, in his "Dictionary of Printing and Printers," 1839. Besides writing for several periodical works, Mr. Chalmers edited "The British Essayists," in 48 vols. 18mo. 1803; an edition of Steevens's Shakspeare, with Life and Notes, 9 vols. 8vo. 1803—1805; A History of the Colleges, &c., of Oxford, 2 vols. 8vo. 1810; an edition of "The English Poets, from Chaucer to Cowper," 21 vols. royal 18mo. 1810. He was also author of an original work, in 3 vols. second edition, 1815, which had previously appeared in the Gentleman's Magazine, intituled "The Projector," a periodical paper, originally published between January 1802 and November 1809. Of this work Mr. Timperley fairly writes that "it successfully seized on the follies and vices of the day; and has displayed in their exposure a large fund of wit, humour, and delicate irony." Mr. Chalmers was a pleasant, convivial companion, which, with his conversational talents, and intimacy with the principal London publishers, secured him a seat at the Hall Dinners of the Stationers' Company at all their public meetings. I met Mr. Chalmers frequently, and ever found him cheerful, communicative, and friendly. He died Dec. 10, 1834, aged 75.

Though George Robinson had succeeded in creating and sustaining the largest bookselling and publishing trade of his time, he failed to provide for his successors that mental organization and machinery which were indispensable for continuing it: conscious that the concern was of his own creating, he seems to have thought that he could not keep the management too exclusively to himself. His son and his brothers he admitted, indeed, into partnership, and assigned to each his place and duties; but they were treated by him rather as agents than principals. He was king and autocrat; and whilst he conceded to them, nominally, the position of equals, in rank, he carefully retained the supreme and ruling power. The consequence became painfully manifest, immediately after his death, in 1801. The surviving partners found themselves engaged in a large and intricate business, of which neither of them knew much beyond the particular department to which his attention had been almost exclusively devoted. Ignorant of the pecuniary position of the house, of the money capital at their disposal for sustaining it, and equally so of the means and method of its proper application, they saw no hope of relief but by a friendly commission of bankruptcy. The affairs were wound up, the property sold, and, to their surprise, it was found that there was enough to satisfy every creditor, in full, with a surplus of £20,000. The surviving partners arose from this painful investigation with their personal credit and honour untarnished, but their commercial importance had departed.

It remains that I now give some account of the Longmans—the first of whom was Thomas, at the sign of "the Ship and Black Swan," whose name appeared to books in 1726, joined with Thomas and John Osborne. He appears to have realized a good fortune, and, dying in 1755, left the property to his widow. She, with the nephew of her first husband, Thomas Longman, conducted the business for some time. They possessed valuable copyrights, in Greek and Latin school-books of the higher class, which, at that time, had a large sale. This nephew was esteemed a tradesman of correct judgment, of great integrity in his dealings, and of kindly disposition. I had opportunities of seeing him occasionally towards the close of his life. He retired from business about 1793, retaining only so much of it as was connected with the sale of the stock belonging to his copyrights, and died at his house at Hampstead in 1797, at the age of 60, greatly esteemed by all who knew him. His eldest son, Thomas Norton Longman, succeeded to the father's business as wholesale and retail bookseller and publisher, on the same plan and scale, his principal assistant being Christopher Brown, the father of my excellent friend, Thomas Brown, who served his apprenticeship to Mr. Longman, and now deservedly occupies the honourable post of a principal partner in the house. In 1797, my eldest brother, Owen Rees, who had been thoroughly trained to business in one of the principal bookselling houses in Bristol, joined Mr. Longman, when the firm was briefly designated, "Longman & Rees." Finding his health declining, in 1837, he determined to close his connexion with the house, and arrangements were made with this view. Before they were concluded, he went to Wales for the removal of what was deemed a temporary indisposition, and on the 5th of September, died, in the 67th year of his age, upon the estate (then his own property) on which he had been born, and where he had hoped to pass some years in tranquil retirement, after the anxieties and fatigues of a long life of arduous and unremitting application to business.

Of this once-amiable and estimable person, I (Britton) avail myself of the present opportunity to put on record an expression of my own warm feelings of attachment and sincere friendship. Intimately acquainted with him for nearly forty years, and often associated in the counting-house, on committees, at the social board, and in other pursuits, I knew him well, and not only respected him for generosity of conduct and sentiment, but for that friendly and kindly disposition he manifested on all occasions. Never was there a man who more fully and truly acted the character of "Harmony" on the great stage of the world, than Owen Rees. In an extensive intercourse with authors and artists, with booksellers and other tradesmen, indeed, with all classes of society, he was bland, courteous, candid, and sincere. In the numerous meetings of the partners in the "Beauties of England," when I was but little known to or by Mr. Rees, and when there were often angry contentions between the booksellers and the authors, I always found him eager and anxious to reconcile differences, to sooth irritated feelings, and endeavour to urge the authors to industry and perseverance, and his colleagues to forbearance and generosity. Such conduct and such manners could not fail to create a friendly feeling in my heart, and, from a more intimate connexion with him afterwards, in consequence of the firm having a share in the "Beauties of Wiltshire," the "Architectural," and the "Cathedral Antiquities," and in others of my literary works, I invariably found a sincere friend in Mr. Rees. Many happy hours have I spent in his company, in Paternoster Row and at my own humble home, and never saw him with a frown on his benignant countenance, nor heard a harsh, ungenerous sentiment from his lips—I loved him, whilst living, and have often lamented his loss, since death has parted us.

In 1804, Thomas Hurst and Cosmo Orme were added to the firm. The story of Thomas Hurst may afford a lesson and warning to speculators, and also to generous-hearted persons, who are susceptible of being imposed on by the seductions of the cunning and crafty. I knew him some years before he joined the firm of Longman and Co., and found him then, as I did in his days of prosperity, kind, friendly, and generous. At first he conducted a business nearly opposite Longman's, and supplied several country booksellers with the London publications. By diligence, devotion to his customers, and obliging manners, he soon augmented his property and profits, and was doing well when he joined the new firm. In this he managed the country department, and was highly esteemd by all who knew him. He was living in an elegant, but unostentatious style, with a carriage and good establishment, on the brow of Highgate Hill, where I have spent many joyful hours in the company of cordial friends. In an evil moment he became connected with an artful and unprincipled man, who was engaged in a good bookselling business in Yorkshire, and who afterwards embarked in a large and daring undertaking in London. John, the elder brother of Thomas Hurst, who was a man of retiring disposition, of unassuming manners, and of punctilious honesty of principle, was partner with the person alluded to, but wholly unfitted for the hazardous game in which he became involved. He was quiescent, whilst his partner was artful and ostentatious. Their capital was soon sunk, and credit was then obtained to a vast extent; for the partner, not satisfied with a large business in books and prints, embarked in building houses, and speculated in hops. The elder Mr. Hurst saw and felt the imminent danger in which he was embarked, and prevailed on his brother to sign accommodation bills to a great amount. He had not courage to refuse, but drew in the name of the firm, of the Row, as he had been accustomed to do in the regular routine of business. Some of these bills were duly paid, but they became so numerous and to such large amounts, that Longman and Co. required an explanation, dissolved the partnership, and bound Mr. T. Hurst to be personally responsible for all further outstanding bills. They also paid to their retiring partner more than forty thousand pounds, his valued share in the house. But even this sum was not enough to meet all the liabilities: whence he became a ruined man. He made two or three efforts to regain credit and business; but these were not to be obtained. The elder brother, John, died broken-hearted; and Thomas was reduced to the mortifying state of seeking an asylum for old age, as an inmate to, and dependant on the charity of the Charter House, in which he died in the year 1850. In consequence of some subsequent changes occasioned by the death of my brother, and later by that of T. N. Longman, the retirement of Hurst and Orme, and the introduction of other persons, to take their places, the firm has assumed its present form of "Longman, Brown, Green, and Longmans." After the introduction of these new partners, of excellent business habits, various new schemes for the enlargement and extension of the trade were carried into execution. Hence, within a short period, the house rose to an importance and reputation which had never before been attained by any similar establishment in the world. To the retail branch they devoted a distinct department, to which was joined a choice and extensive library of old books. This was a novelty in a publishing house, and I believe that it originated in obtaining a large collection of scarce and curious books, on old Poetry and the Drama, which the partners had purchased, for a very large sum, from Thomas Hill. The event was at a time when Bibliomania was raging in London,—when certain noblemen and gentlemen were in the habit of attending sales, and competing for large and tall-paper books, and for rare copies, many of which had become so from their worthlesseness. A remarkable Catalogue, called "Bibliotheca Anglo-Poetica," of the Hill library, was prepared in 1816 by——Griffiths, a clerk in Longman's house, and secured much praise from the book-buyers, and the learned in black-letter lore, for the knowledge and tact it manifested. Thence forward, for many years, the house continued to purchase largely at sales, and from individuals, either libraries or collections of books, and occasionally issued catalogues. After the death of Mr. Griffiths, his place was supplied by Mr. Reader; but within the last few years the whole collection was sold by public auction. I am not a little surprised and mortified to look over the pages, and meagre Index, of the Rev. Dr. Dibdin's "Reminiscences," in vain, for some notice of T. Hill, and Mr. Griffith's "Bibliotheca." The general wholesale trade, for the supply of country booksellers in the British Isles, and for the foreign markets, surpassed that of all preceding establishments; whilst the publishing business, if it cannot be said to have gone beyond that of any other British house, was unquestionably inferior to none.

In adverting to the publications of this firm, it is curious to observe one name of some eminence in literature and science, which has been in association with Longman and Co. for more than 120 years. This is Ephraim Chambers, the author, or editor, of the original "Cyclopædia," which work was first published by subscription in 1728, in two volumes, folio. It soon acquired great popularity, and attained a second edition in 1738. The author, finding his health impaired by literary labours, went to France, in hopes of recruiting his mental and bodily strength, and at the same time collecting materials for his projected book. I have in my possession some interesting letters written by him during this tour, addressed to his publisher. The "Cyclopædia" was reprinted under his superintendence in 1739, and was his last literary effort. His constitution gave way, and he died in May, 1740. The work was again reprinted in 1741, and also in 1746, when it was thought desirable to add a Supplement, to embrace the more modern discoveries in science and in the arts. This Supplement, prepared by Dr. Hill, and Mr. G. L. Scott, was published in 1753, in two folio volumes. After an interval of some years, the work still maintaining a high reputation, the proprietors projected a new edition, incorporating the Supplement, together with new matter of importance. Some difficulty was experienced in finding a suitable editor. At last Dr. Abraham Rees was chosen, who was then mathematical tutor at a dissenting college in London, and had acquired considerable reputation for his scientific knowledge and literary talents. The first number, in folio, was published in 1778, and the work was continued weekly till completed, in 418 numbers, forming four large volumes, with numerous prints. The current sale for many years amounted to 5000 numbers weekly, and there was a large demand for the work, in this form, for a long time after its completion. At length it was found expedient to publish another edition, or rather an entirely new work, under the same title, and under the same learned and laborious editor, who called to his aid a number of writers holding high rank in the several important departments of science. The work received the designation of the "New Cyclopædia." It was published periodically, in parts, or half volumes, and appeared regularly till completed in 40 volumes. The publication, which commenced in 1802, occupied about sixteen years; but the labour of the indefatigable editor, including the period of preparation, extended over twenty years, measured, as he said, not by fragments of time, but by whole days, of twelve and fourteen hours each. In the general preface, the editor has given the names of his principal coadjutors, and I find your name recorded in the list, in connexion with the subjects of antiquities, topography, &c., upon which you furnished many valuable articles.

I had the gratification of introducing the following gentlemen to the firm, to write articles on subjects connected with their professional studies: E. W. Brayley, who wrote on Enamelling; T. Phillips, R.A., on Painting; and Sharon Turner, on English History. The last gentleman became intimate with the partners, was employed by them for many years afterwards, and attained great popularity and handsome remuneration for his historical works, through the medium of such publishers.

Reminiscences respecting this once important work, and its phalanx of contributors, in art, literature, and science—of their frequent intercourse at the Soirées which the publishers established at their great book manufactory and mart, No. 39,

&c., Paternoster Row—are impressed on my memory and feelings with intense pleasure, mixed with some painful emotions of having for ever lost the converse and excitement which emanated from the friendly and intellectual collision, then and there produced. The respectable firm of Longman and Co. not only invited and assembled nearly all the contributors to the "Cyclopædia," periodically for several successive winters, but were in the habit of calling many of them together around the social and splendid dining table, where the acknowledged professors of literature and art met, on equal and friendly terms, eminent amateurs of both. Such unions were novelties in England, and I believe, in Europe; and were eminently calculated to foster good feelings, and promote harmony and intimacy between persons in different gradations of trade, literature, art, and science. Hence friendships were made; new discoveries were proclaimed; opinions, public measures, and the conduct of public men, canvassed; courtesies and civilities were exchanged between persons whose studies and pursuits were often in rivalry, and human amenities were cultivated. In such company, and under such influences, I own that I not only felt elated and proud, but substantially benefited, both mentally and morally. The amiable and benignant editor of the "Cyclopædia," who often formed one of these parties, seemed, to my fancy, something above humanity: for never was there a man more deservedly beloved and respected than the Rev. Dr. Abraham Rees.

Besides giving to the editor the assistance and co-operation of eminent writers in literature and science, the proprietors spared no expense to provide artists of the first talents for its illustrations. Among those who furnished drawings, were Howard, Landseer, Donovan, Russell, Opie, Ottley, Phillips, and Farey; while among the engravers, were Milton, Lowry, and Scott. The "New Cyclopædia" was in all respects a great and important undertaking. It embodied writings by some of the most distinguished scientific men of the age, on subjects of primary consequence, and it involved an expense almost unexampled in the history of literature: the pecuniary outlay could not have been less than 300,000 pounds sterling.

Another literary speculation of considerable importance, undertaken in 1803, was the "Annual Review," intended to comprise, in one large volume, an account of the entire English literature of each year. The editorship was committed to Arthur Aikin, whose scientific and literary attainments eminently fitted him for such an office. He was ably assisted by the distinguished members of his own family, and by many persons of note in the literary world: among whom may be mentioned, in theology, the Rev. Chas. Wellbeloved, of York; in natural history, the late Rev. Wm. Wood, of Leeds; and in general literature, Robert Southey, and William Taylor, of Norwich. The numerous letters by Taylor and Southey, in "A Memoir of the Life and Writings" of the former, 2 vols. 8vo., by J. W. Robberds, are truly interesting, as calculated to unfold some of the mysteries and fascinations of authorship and reviewing, as well as characterising two writers, whose works produced many and great effects in the world of literature, between the years 1793 and 1836. Though not much known to the reading community, Mr. Taylor was an extraordinary writer; and from the number and variety of his criticisms and essays, in the "Monthly Magazine," the "Monthly Review," the "Annual Review," the "Anthenæum,". in magazines, and other periodicals, he must have produced strong and important results on the readers of his works. The work was conducted by Mr. Aikin for six years, when, in consequence of new arrangements in the management of the literary concern of the house, I undertook to prepare the seventh volume. In this arduous task I was materially aided by most of the gentlemen who had lent their service to my esteemed predecessor, and I had the gratification of receiving a valuable contribution from Walter Scott, on a subject, for the treatment of which he was perhaps the fittest writer of the age;—"Ancient Romance." With the seventh volume the work ceased.

In the year 1807, Longman and Co. entered on the publication of a new periodical, called "The Anthenæum," under the editorship of Dr. Aikin, in competition with the "Monthly Magazine," which had been commenced a few years before by Mr. R. Phillips, of St. Paul's Churchyard. This publication consisted of monthly numbers, at one shilling each, was continued to the close of the seventh half-yearly volume, and, under the able editorship of Dr. Aikin, assisted by the contributions of various members of his own family, with Dr. Enfield, and other persons of distinction in literature, had acquired great popularity. The projector was at the time regarded as a sufferer from his political principles; and Dr. Aikin, with other friends to liberal opinions in politics, readily espoused his cause, and lent their talents to assist him. No sooner, however, had the magazine obtained an extensive circulation, than Phillips took the entire management, and dispensed with the services of his first friend. The magazine, however, if it lost from this cause much of the literary excellence and refinement which had characterized the earlier numbers, retained, by his judicious selection of miscellaneous matters of general interest, its hold of the popular mind, and commanded a very extensive sale. It occurred to Longmans that a magazine, which should be devoted to topics of a higher literary character, might be successful; and under this conviction they projected the periodical above-mentioned, under the title of "The Athenæum." The work included contributions by Dr. Falconer, of Bath, and Mr. Dewhurst, of London; Robert Southey,—Bland, Elton, and many others. On this periodical I had the pleasure of acting as sub-editor, and furnished for it most of the larger articles of obituary. But the sale did not yield an adequate return to compensate the publishers, and the work was on that account relinquished.

Not long after the discontinuance of the "Athenæum," the house embarked in an undertaking of great magnitude and expense, entitled "The British Gallery of Pictures," which was intended to consist of fine engravings from the best works of the old masters, in the private collections of English noblemen, &c., some of the prints being coloured in imitation of the originals. In the plan of this work two objects were embraced:—firstly, small prints, including all the pictures in certain celebrated collections; and, secondly, copies of a selected number only of the more important and admired works. The latter prints were on a larger scale than the former, some being of the actual size of the original pictures. Each series was accompanied by appropriate letter-press, and the prints in both cases were coloured. Eminent artists were employed to copy the pictures for engraving, as well as to colour the prints. Among the engravers were Cardon, Schiavonetti, and other able artists; and, whilst the artistic arrangements were entrusted to Tomkins, the literary department was confided to Henry Tresham, R.A., and W. Y. Ottley; both gentlemen being well qualified for their respective duties. An immense outlay was incurred upon this work, which was carried on for some years with great spirit; but it proved to be a very profitable speculation, and was brought to a premature close, when the only portion really finished was the Cleveland-house collection, in one volume, folio. The water-colour drawings from the original pictures had been exhibited to the public in a gallery specially appropriated to them in Bond Street; and, on the termination of the work, the proprietors obtained an Act of Parliament to dispose of the pictures, with the engravings, by lottery.

But whilst the house thus employed a large capital, in the production of what may be termed periodical works, it was liberal in the appropriation of other portions to standard books, on important literary subjects, by authors of the most distinguished reputation. Amongst these were the Aikins, Scott, Moore, and Southey. Complaints have often been made of the sordid spirit of booksellers, and their inadequate remuneration of authors. No doubt writers are often very badly paid for works upon which they have bestowed much time, labour, and talent; and the cause of literature has, it may be believed, suffered on this account. But I am quite sure the evil has not always originated with publishers, who, like other tradesmen, give for the material the amount which they deem it to be worth in respect to the profit it is likely to yield. Generally, I believe—and I speak from a long experience—the booksellers act with commendable liberality. A reference to a list of prices given by Lintot to authors, early in the last century—a curious document, printed by Nichols, and now in my possession—shows that authors, at that time, were handsomely paid. In well-known instances, booksellers of a later date,—the Robinsons, the Dillys, the Johnsons, the Cadells, the Murrays, and lastly the Longmans,—have dealt most liberally by authors, and on some occasions have given sums of large, not to say exorbitant amount, for manuscripts, on the bare supposition that the returns might justify the expenditure, and yield a fair trading profit. In my personal knowledge, I can say that the firm, now alluded to, always acted in such transactions with great and generous spirit.

At a later period, Oct. 1802, Longman and Co. became part-proprietors and London publishers of the "Edinburgh Review." This produced them an important accession of literary friends of eminent abilities, among whom were Walter Scott, Rev. Sidney Smith, Francis Jeffrey, Henry Brougham, Francis Horner, James Mill, and others.

About this time they became connected also with John Pinkerton, the author of "General Geography," which appeared first in three, and afterwards in two quarto volumes. It was a work of great labour, being written and compiled from the best authorities in the European languages, and illustrated by numerous maps, engraved by Lowry. Pinkerton also prepared a large "General Atlas," a well-executed folio volume; and, more especially, a "Collection of Voyages and Travels," in sixteen quarto volumes, with prints by the Cookes and others. These large and costly works were the joint property of Longman and Co. and Cadell and Davies. Pinkerton was a singular and degraded man. I (Britton) was made too well acquainted with him for my own reputation and for my own domestic comforts. He rented, and occupied, for a short time, a house, No. 9, Tavistock Place, next door to my own. His home was frequently a place of popular disturbance, by females whom he had married, or lived with, and deserted. When in want of money, or over-excited by drink, they knocked at his door, broke the windows, and otherwise behave riotously. He was a disreputable character; and though he had been most liberally paid by Longman's house, he went to Paris in the latter part of his life, and died in poverty in 1826. He was an author of several works, in poetry, history, geography, criticism; all of which, says the writer in "The Penny Cyclopædia," "with all their faults, not only overflow with curious learning and research, but bear upon them the impression of a vigorous, an ingenious, and even an original mind. His violence and dogmatism, his arrogance and self-conceit, his pugnacity and contempt for all who dissented from his views, but above all, his shallow and petulant attacks upon the common creed in religion and morals, have raised a general prejudice against Pinkerton, which has prevented justice being done to his acquirements and talents." Mr. Dawson Turner possesses a large collection of his correspondence, from which two octavo volumes have been published, but not much to the credit of the Scotchman. A later speculation, on a large scale, published by Longman's house, was "Lardner's Cabinet Cyclopædia," in small 12mo., extending to 133 volumes; for which many distinguished writers were engaged, and heavy expenses were incurred.

For several years it was the custom of the firm to give Dinners at certain intervals, when the partners assembled around their hospitable board a number of authors and artists of high reputation; and, besides these more limited réunions, they opened the house in Paternoster Row, one evening in the week, during several seasons, for a Soirée, which was rendered easily accessible to persons of literary tastes, and from all countries.

I come now to the third Class of booksellers who chiefly dealt in retail; whose traffic was mostly with their brother tradesmen, whom they supplied with a single copy, or several copies of books, at what was called the trade price, which produced them only a small profit. Paternoster Row contained, at that time, several respectable booksellers of this class. Mr. Bladon's shop was the well-known depository of old plays. You may remember to have seen, some years ago, in Leadenhall Street, a large hardware warehouse, which attracted the notice of all passengers by its filthy appearance, both on the outside and the inside. The proprietor was scarcely less notorious on account of his dingy aspect, which obtained for him the designation of "Dirty Dick." Bladon was greatly respected as a tradesman, but his shop might have rivalled the Leadenhall Street repository for its affluence in dust and soot. The next to be noticed is Symonds, who carried on a large business in the sale of periodicals, which he purchased in quantities, as they were published, and sold singly, or in small numbers to booksellers' collectors, at the wholesale prices. By this plan the trade was greatly accommodated, and his own interest promoted. He pursued the same course with respect to the more popular pamphlets of the day. In times of great political agitation, such as those in which he lived, this practice of publishing for authors was not without danger, as Symonds had the misfortune to experience. One tract, to which he had permitted his name to be attached, who pronounced a libel; and he had to endure the penalty by an imprisonment of some months in Newgate, where I once visited him. He died in middle life, greatly respected. The business of this house was afterwards conducted on the same scale and plan, by Mr. Sherwood, who had been Mr. Symonds' active and valuable assistant. Contiguous to this shop was that of Parsons, who sold books and pamphlets upon the same plan, but on a less extensive scale. He was occasionally a publisher, on his own account. His chief speculation was an edition of Hume and Smollett's "History of England," in 18mo., which, like that by Cooke, was embellished with prints and portraits.

Thomas Evans, though advanced in age, ranked among the retail booksellers of the Row. He was originally a porter to Johnson, a bookseller of Ludgate Street, and succeeded to the business of Howes, Clarke, and Collins, by which he obtained respectability and a good fortune. The bulk of his property he bequeathed to Charles, father of the present T. Brown, already noticed. In his will, he directs that his funeral expenses do not exceed forty shillings. In early life he acted as the publisher of the "Morning Chronicle," which first appeared in 1770, and in that capacity had the misfortune to offend Oliver Goldsmith, who went to the office and unceremoniously assailed Evans with a stick. The sturdy Welshman, however, soon recovered from his surprise, and with one blow laid the poet prostrate on the floor. Another of the retail booksellers of this period was John Walker, who for some time officiated as (what was called) the "Trade Auctioneer." He was greatly respected by his neighbours. In the latter part of his life his name was familiar to the public as publisher of Dr. Wolcot's, alias Peter Pindar's, works. It is a common adage that there are "secrets in all trades;" and it is well known that every craft and calling has its peculiar customs, privileges, and technicalities of language. A few of the large wholesale publishers of London are in the habit of making up, either annually or occasionally, what are called "trade sales;" when they prepare a catalogue of their large stock books, and distribute it to a select number of retail dealers, who are invited to meet the publisher and his auctioneer at a certain tavern, where, after partaking of an early dinner, the "trade auctioneer" proceeds to dispose of the works named in the catalogue, to the parties present. The various lots comprise many copies of recently-published works, and are offered and sold at rather less than the usual trade prices;

the purchasers being, moreover, allowed to give bills, at three, at four, eight, twelve, and sixteen months, according to the amount they buy, or take a moderate discount for cash. Hence have originated two great evils in the bookselling business; namely, the encouragement to print large editions of books, from the facility of disposing of them at reduced prices, and the depreciation of those works in the public market, by copies being offered at such sales much below their original prices. Mr. Walker, I believe, was amongst the first trade auctioneers, and was followed by Mr. Saunders, a prompt, off-hand man, whose language and peculiarity of manners are humorously burlesqued in "Chalcographiomania." The celebrated William Hone was for a short time auctioneer to the trade, but was irregular in his accounts, whence arose many embarrassments in after life. Two large stock-holders of books have since become their own salesmen, on these occasions: both eminently qualified, from promptitude of thought and action, and extensive knowledge of business. The late Thomas Tegg of the "Poultry," when I first knew him, kept a small shop in St. John's Street, for pamphlets, songs, &c. Thence he removed to Cheapside, where he accumulated a large stock of books, and established an evening auction. He afterwards took the old Mansion-house in the Poultry, and progressively published numerous books. Having settled one of his sons in Australia, he thereby obtained a channel for the sale of large editions of cheap books, and deemed it expedient to adopt the practice of some of the great publishing firms, by making up an annual sale, and acting as auctioneer. My friend, Mr. H. G. Bohn, has followed the same track, and has astonished the Metropolitan traders in' literature by the stock brought forward, the rapidity of dispatch, and the novelties he has introduced into this branch of London business. Mr. Hodgson, of Fleet Street, is at present the confidential and respected agent of the London publishers. The poems of Peter Pindar, this once noted and powerful satirist, were extensively read at the end of the last century. They were, however, very dear to the purchaser, being printed in thin quarto pamphlets at 2s. 6d. each, and containing only a very small portion of letter-press. His first attacks, in 1782, were the Royal Academicians, some of whom he assailed with bitter satire, sarcasm, and irony. King George the Third was next vituperated, in a poem called "The Lousiad," descriptive of the circumstances of an animal, unnamable to "ears polite," being seen on the plate of the monarch at a royal dinner. For some years the author continued to publish his philippes against artists, royal and noble personages, and also on some authors; one of whom, Wm. Gifford, who had written the "Baviad and Mæviad," a poem, in which many of the authors of the time were severely castigated, also wielded his galled pen against the morals and poetry of Dr. Wolcot. This castigation was so stringent and caustic that the Doctor was provoked to seek his lampooner in the shop of Mr. Wright, a political publisher, of Piccadilly. Thither Peter repaired, with a stout cudgel in hand, determined to inflict a summary and severe chastisement on his literary opponent. Gifford was a small and weak person; Wolcot was large, and strengthened by passion, but he was a coward, and after a short personal struggle was turned into the street by two or three persons, then in the shop. Gifford afterwards wrote and printed an "Epistle to Peter Pindar," with an "Introduction and Postscript," 1800, in which he dealt out a most virulent and unqualified tirade against the Doctor. It acquired great popularity, and in a few weeks attained a third edition. The pamphlet has not any publisher's name. This was the second victory which Gifford had achieved over literary opponents; a former being Anthony Pas-

event was related to me by the Poet. A good account of his life is given in the "Penny Cyclopædia." Mr. Cyrus Redding, who had been familiar with Wolcot for many years, gave some interesting anecdotes of him in the "New Monthly Magazine," vols. 17 and 19; and has recently written further notice in "The Athenæum" for May and June 1852, to correct certain mis-statements in Jerdan's "Auto-Biography." Wolcot died in Somers-Town, Jan. 13, 1807, in the 81st year of his age, and was buried at St. Paul's, Covent Garden.

Mr. Bent was a bookseller of long standing in the Row, but he was chiefly known as the publisher of that very useful work, the "London Catalogue of Books," first printed in 1799, which is still continued monthly by Mr. T. Hodgson. This gentleman is also editor of "The London Catalogue of Books, published in Great Britain, with their Sizes, Prices, and Publishers' Names, from 1814 to 1846," 8vo. 1846; and "Bibliotheca Londinensis: a Classified Index to the Literature of Great Britain during Thirty Years," 8vo. 1848. Bent also published "The Universal Magazine," a periodical which at one time had an extensive sale.

I may conclude my list of retail booksellers with the names of the Wilkies, brothers, who were long respected inhabitants of the Row. With their retail business they carried on a wholesale trade of some extent in supplying country booksellers. One of the brothers, Thomas Wilkie, trafficked also in the public securities, and kept an office for the sale of lottery tickets. He removed to Salisbury, where I became acquainted with him, 1798, and found him obliging and kindly disposed. Amongst other things, he told me that on the first performance of Sheridan's play of "The Rivals," which the Wilkies published, the author was so scantily supplied with wardrobe, that he borrowed a shirt of Mr. W.'s father to witness the first acting of his own play, but forgot to return the said shirt; as he did also a few guineas, which he had borrowed of the same party.

In Ave Maria Lane, the firm of Scatcherd and Letterman carried on a large wholesale country business. Amongst other works they published, was "London and its Environs, or the General Ambulator." The 12th edition, 1820, greatly enlarged and improved by Mr. Brayley, is now before me, and is a very useful work, though supplanted by the justly-popular publications by Charles Knight: "Pictorial London," 6 vols. 1841. In the same lane, the house of Law was chiefly noted for school-books. An apprentice, and afterwards managing clerk, in that business, was Peter

Courtier, whose partiality for poetry induced him to write and publish a volume of "Verses," some of which had appeared in periodicals. He was the first mover, in and an active supporter of "the School of Eloquence."

The Laws were succeeded by the Whittakers, whose active exertions and skill in business speedily increased it to a great extent. Amongst many of their publications, was one in five volumes, by Miss Mitford, called "Our Village," which has passed through several editions, and is justly admired for the vivid fancy, the pathos, and amiable sympathy which pervade its pages. This work is now brought into two volumes by Mr. H. G. Bohn, and issued in his popular series of books. She first appeared as a poet in 1810. The reader will find some pleasing, and justly complimentary, remarks on Miss Mitford's writings, in a recently published and interesting volume, "A Journal of Summer-time in the Country," by the Rev. R. A. Willmott. Second edition, 1832.

William Pinnock was author of a long list of books, which, though little known in the literary world, have been of great value in the advancement of education and knowledge. All his writings have been adapted and addressed to the juvenile age, and have been peculiarly calculated to "teach the young idea how to shoot," and tempt it to pursue the path of learning with pleasantry and even fascination. By "The London Catalogue from 1814 to 1846," I see that Pinnock has produced twelve volumes of Catechisms, eight of Histories, and twenty-two others on Grammar, Languages, Arithmetic, Geography, Poetry, &c. These books have all been very popular and profitable to the publishers, though the author has, like too many other improvident ones, known the galling pressure of indigence.

Near Mr. Law's house, was the printing and publishing establishment of J. Wilkes, who became well known by the "Encyclopædia Londinensis," with numerous engravings, a work which extended to twenty-six volumes, at £63, and had a considerable sale. The names of Wilkes, Ave-Maria Lane, and Encyclopædia Londinensis, are indelibly impressed on my (Britton's) memory. On my first visit to Salisbury, in 1798, I assumed the title, or rather it was forced upon me, of Artist; and Mr. Easton, a bookseller and printer of the city, asked me to make a drawing of Salisbury Cathedral, to be engraved for, and published in, the great "national work" above-named. My ambition was aroused, but I was terrified; for I knew not how or where to begin, nor how or in what manner I was to proceed, even if I dared undertake such a herculean task. I was impelled to try; had pencils, rulers, and a table placed opposite the middle of the North chief transept. With the print from Price's "Survey," from the same point, before me, I sketched, and scratched, and rubbed out; and continued thus occupied for three successive days, with several persons looking on, and wondering at my temerity and incompetency. Often have I reflected on this scene and event; and more than once have I heard friends, who were there, remark on the exhibition, and their astonishment at seeing afterwards a tolerably-executed engraving from the sketch then made.

In Stationers' Court was the warehouse of B. Crosby, one of the original partners in the "Beauties of England and Wales," who had a very extensive country business, which has for some years been conducted by Simpkin and Marshall. Though not distinguished as publishers, this firm carries on the largest business in the book-trade of any house in Europe, and is only rivalled perhaps by the Harpers, of New York. The only daughter of the late Mr. Simpkin is the wife of the most enterprising and energetic publisher and bookseller of this metropolis, Henry G. Bohn, whose Catalogue of Books of 1841 is unprecedented for the number, value, and variety of its articles. It extends to no less than 1948 octavo pages.

This paved Court is associated with my own personal and topographical reminiscences too memorably to be passed unnoticed. In this central part of London, resided John, Duke of Bretagne and Earl of Richmond, during the reigns of Edwards II. and III., in a large mansion which was afterwards occupied by an Earl of Pembroke, and called Pembroke's Inn. It was afterwards possessed by the Company of Stationers, who rebuilt it of wood. That was burnt in the great fire of London, after which the present plain, tasteless Hall was erected. According to Clarendon, the stationers' property then destroyed was valued at £200,000. Here the Company of Stationers hold their courts, transact their business, register and deposit books, and assemble frequently at the festive board. At two of the Master's feasts I have been a guest, and enjoyed the company, conversation, and civic repasts with much zest. The Portraits preserved here remind us of names and literary works which have excited our curiosity and gratified our feelings in early reading days. These are of Richardson, Prior, Steele, Hoadly, Nelson, Dryden, Alderman Boydell, and others.

The first was one of the Masters of the Company, and had his wife painted for the place, to keep him company. Leigh Hunt, speaking of these portraits says, that representing the author of Clarissa Harlowe represents him as a "sensitive, enduring man—a heap of bad nerves." He further remarks, that Hoadly, "looks at once jovial and decided, like a good-natured controversialist." Concerts, as well as dinners, were frequently performed in this hall. Odes and other pieces were written for such occasions. Amongst these, Dryden's "Song for Saint Cecilia's Day," was produced in 1687; and, ten years afterwards, "Alexander's Feast" was written, composed, and performed: the composer being Jeremiah Clarke, who shot himself "for love." Though the Hall and Company of Stationers are associated with pleasant memories, persons, and events, there are others which tend to lower both in my own estimation. From the commencement of my (Britton's) literary career to the present time, I have been obliged (by Act of Parliament) to present one copy of every book which I have written and published to this company. This is the only London Company whose members are restricted to their own craft. It is called, "The Mystery or Art of the Stationers." For many years the said Stationers assumed the exclusive privilege of publishing all the almanacs of the country, and produced many which were frivolous and illiterate in style and matter. To counteract these, Charles Knight projected and published, for "The Society for the Diffusion of Useful Knowledge," in 1828, "The British Almanac," which has become eminently and justly popular, and has also superseded most of the almanacs which disseminated astrological nonsense and literary absurdity. The reader will find a very interesting paper on the history and characteristics of almanacs in "The Companion to the British Almanac," for 1829; also in "The London Magazine," for December, 1828.

Proceeding to the northwest corner of St. Paul's Churchyard, we recognize a name associated with the earliest recollections of youthful readers,— that of Newberry, who, after Carnan, furnished the largest and most interesting contributions to the juvenile libraries of the country. On the death of Newberry, his widow continued the business aided by John Harris, who afterwards became her successor. He was in turn succeeded by his son, who soon transferred the business to the present firm of Grant and Griffiths.

Francis Newberry, a member of the above-mentioned family, had a house on the east side of the Churchyard, near Cheapside, where he sold Dr.

The first was one of the Masters of the Company, and had his wife painted for the place, to keep him company. Leigh Hunt, speaking of these portraits says, that representing the author of Clarissa Harlowe represents him as a "sensitive, enduring man—a heap of bad nerves." He further remarks, that Hoadly, "looks at once jovial and decided, like a good-natured controversialist." Concerts, as well as dinners, were frequently performed in this hall. Odes and other pieces were written for such occasions. Amongst these, Dryden's "Song for Saint Cecilia's Day," was produced in 1687; and, ten years afterwards, "Alexander's Feast" was written, composed, and performed: the composer being Jeremiah Clarke, who shot himself "for love." Though the Hall and Company of Stationers are associated with pleasant memories, persons, and events, there are others which tend to lower both in my own estimation. From the commencement of my (Britton's) literary career to the present time, I have been obliged (by Act of Parliament) to present one copy of every book which I have written and published to this company. This is the only London Company whose members are restricted to their own craft. It is called, "The Mystery or Art of the Stationers." For many years the said Stationers assumed the exclusive privilege of publishing all the almanacs of the country, and produced many which were frivolous and illiterate in style and matter. To counteract these, Charles Knight projected and published, for "The Society for the Diffusion of Useful Knowledge," in 1828, "The British Almanac," which has become eminently and justly popular, and has also superseded most of the almanacs which disseminated astrological nonsense and literary absurdity. The reader will find a very interesting paper on the history and characteristics of almanacs in "The Companion to the British Almanac," for 1829; also in "The London Magazine," for December, 1828.

Proceeding to the northwest corner of St. Paul's Churchyard, we recognize a name associated with the earliest recollections of youthful readers,—that of Newberry, who, after Carnan, furnished the largest and most interesting contributions to the juvenile libraries of the country. On the death of Newberry, his widow continued the business aided by John Harris, who afterwards became her successor. He was in turn succeeded by his son, who soon transferred the business to the present firm of Grant and Griffiths.

Francis Newberry, a member of the above-mentioned family, had a house on the east side of the Churchyard, near Cheapside, where he sold Dr.

sister, Mrs. Barbauld, by his friend, Dr. Wm. Enfield, also by Godwin, Holcroft, and many other writers. Johnson at first published this periodical, as agent for Phillips; and his extensive connexion enabled him to promote its success. The speculative proprietor was, however, soon induced to open a small shop for himself, and about the same time he also undertook the task of editing his magazine; thus dispensing with the services of two of his best friends. The "Monthly" rapidly increased in popularity and profit, and for many years continued to be a valuable property. Phillips published numerous other works, chiefly educational; many of which were written by himself, but appeared under the names of popular authors; who probably revised the proofs, and allowed their names to be attached, for a pecuniary consideration. Like his competitors, Phillips published an "Encyclopædia," professedly under the editorship of Dr. Gregory; but which was in fact mostly written by Jeremiah Joyce, whose varied scientific attainments were most inadequately appreciated. In the year 1807, this enterprising publisher served as one of the Sheriffs of London, and discharged the duties of that important office with zeal, energy, and great credit. During this period he was knighted, on presenting an address on behalf of the ministers. In the latter part of his career he suffered severely by the panic, and was obliged to surrender his business to his creditors. Besides numerous original papers in "The Monthly Magazine," Sir Richard was also author of the following literary works: "A Letter to the Livery of London, on the Office of Sheriff," 8vo. 1808; "On the Powers and Duties of Juries, and on the Criminal Laws of England," 8vo. 1811; "A Morning's Walk from London to Kew," 8vo. 1817; "Golden Rules of Social Philosophy, or a New System of Practical Ethics," 8vo. 1826; "A Personal Tour Through the United Kingdom," 8vo. 1828. It is also stated that he originated and published numerous treatises on "The Interrogatory System," in school education, which has proved eminently successful. He was likewise author of "Twelve Essays on the Proximate Causes of the Universe," being a reformed system of natural philosophy; substituting matter and motion for what he called "the silly superstitions and fancies" of attraction, repulsion, &c. These works abound with originality of thought, expressed in terse and pungent language. Though the "Walk to Kew" and the "Personal Tour" do not contain much topographical and antiquarian information, they tempt the reader to accompany and sympathize with the writer, by the fund of anecdote, vivid description, and shrewdness of commentary, which pervade every page. In reading these works, the young student cannot fail to regard the author amongst the philosophers and moralists of his age and country. Sir Richard was a native of London, where he was born in 1767, and died at Brighton, April 1st, 1840. He thus writes to me from Brighton in April 1838, two years before his decease: "Your friendly letter was a ray of sunshine on a very dull day. You struck out for yourself a path of literary renown, and I am quite sure you have reached the summit. For my own part, my pursuits have been so diversified for the last twenty years, that I had almost forgotten one of my youngest literary children—'The Walk to Kew.' Your approbation I value, because on such a subject you are a first-rate judge. You must have read fifty such works: I never read one; and therefore, in my mind, there is no element of comparison. I had no design of the book when I took the walk; and my notes were very scanty. Had it been republished with a dozen good engravings, it might have become popular. Another volume might have been devoted to Hampton Court, and a third to Windsor."

The name and house of Carrington Bowles, on

the north side of St. Paul's Churchyard, were noted for the number and variety of popular Prints which were distributed thence all over the country at the end of the last and beginning of the present century. "Death and the Lady," a figure half skeleton, half female—"Keep within compass," a beau with cocked hat, scarlet coat, &c., standing between the two legs of a pair of compasses, and other showy, admonitory pictures, were to be seen in the farm-houses and cottages in Wiltshire, in my youth-days, whence the names of publisher and place were impressed on the young mind. The late Mr. C. Bowles, on retiring from business with a handsome fortune, built a large villa or mansion at Enfield, on the bank of the New River, and called it Myddleton House, in compliment to the adventurous speculator in that important undertaking. Mr. Bowles's ancestor possessed shares in the New River Company, which were bequeathed to the son, who for many years was an active member of that company. He was a Fellow of the Society of Antiquaries and took great interest in its weekly meetings.

Charles Dilly, of the Poultry, was the survivor of two brothers, who published largely, and accumulated handsome fortunes. On relinquishing business, he was succeeded by Joseph Mawman,

writer, by the fund of anecdote, vivid description, and shrewdness of commentary, which pervade every page. In reading these works, the young student cannot fail to regard the author amongst the philosophers and moralists of his age and country. Sir Richard was a native of London, where he was born in 1767, and died at Brighton, April 1st, 1840. He thus writes to me from Brighton in April 1838, two years before his decease: "Your friendly letter was a ray of sunshine on a very dull day. You struck out for yourself a path of literary renown, and I am quite sure you have reached the summit. For my own part, my pursuits have been so diversified for the last twenty years, that I had almost forgotten one of my youngest literary children—'The Walk to Kew.' Your approbation I value, because on such a subject you are a first-rate judge. You must have read fifty such works: I never read one; and therefore, in my mind, there is no element of comparison. I had no design of the book when I took the walk; and my notes were very scanty. Had it been republished with a dozen good engravings, it might have become popular. Another volume might have been devoted to Hampton Court, and a third to Windsor."

The name and house of Carrington Bowles, on

the north side of St. Paul's Churchyard, were noted for the number and variety of popular Prints which were distributed thence all over the country at the end of the last and beginning of the present century. "Death and the Lady," a figure half skeleton, half female—"Keep within compass," a beau with cocked hat, scarlet coat, &c., standing between the two legs of a pair of compasses, and other showy, admonitory pictures, were to be seen in the farm-houses and cottages in Wiltshire, in my youth-days, whence the names of publisher and place were impressed on the young mind. The late Mr. C. Bowles, on retiring from business with a handsome fortune, built a large villa or mansion at Enfield, on the bank of the New River, and called it Myddleton House, in compliment to the adventurous speculator in that important undertaking. Mr. Bowles's ancestor possessed shares in the New River Company, which were bequeathed to the son, who for many years was an active member of that company. He was a Fellow of the Society of Antiquaries and took great interest in its weekly meetings.

Charles Dilly, of the Poultry, was the survivor of two brothers, who published largely, and accumulated handsome fortunes. On relinquishing business, he was succeeded by Joseph Mawman, of York, who afterwards removed to Ludgate Street, where he was succeeded by Mr. Fellows. Mr. Mawman published "An Excursion to the Highlands of Scotland," &c., 8vo. 1805, which contains two prints from drawings by Turner.

The firm of Vernor and Hood had removed the business from Birchin Lane to the Poultry, where they published many literary works, and with whom I (Britton) commenced my literary career as a Topographer. My business and personal connections with that House involve reminiscences of persons, books, and events, which would afford matter for a moderately-sized volume. From the year 1799 to 1810, I was in almost constant communication with Mr. Hood, who was the managing partner, and who was an active, persevering, punctilious man of business. The House attained considerable distinction in the literary world by the publication of Bloomfeld's "Farmer's Boy," and other volumes of poems by the rustic, self-educated author—by the exuberant praises of Capel Lofft—by the publication of "The Monthly Mirror," under the editorship of Edward Dubois and Thomas Hill—by "The Poetical Magazine," edited by David Carey, who had published "The Pleasures of Nature," with other poetry, novels, &c. Among many works which issued from this firm was "The Beauties of Wiltshire" and "The Beauties of England and Wales," with the accompanying "British Atlas." In 1808 the House acquired much notoriety by a trial in the Court of King's Bench, when Sir John Carr brought an action-at-law against these publishers for a libel on himself and his literary works. This author had obtained much reputation for his Tours in France, in the North, in Holland, in Ireland, &c., and has been rewarded by different publishers with nearly two thousand pounds for copyrights. His "Tour in Holland," one volume 4to, 1807, which was purchased and published by Sir Richard Phillips, was turned into ridicule by Edward Dubois, in a sportive, ironical, and satirical small volume, entitled "My Pocket Book," written in a fluent, anecdotical, gossiping style. The "Tours" were much read and abundantly commented on by the regular reviews and by daily journals. The author obtained fame and fortune, when the witty and caustic satire alluded to provoked him and the publisher to prosecute the writer of "My Pocket Book." A verdict was given, in behalf of the liberty of the press, against the plaintiff, who was non-suited, and driven from the court in disgrace. A full account of the trial was published, with several letters from the Earl of Mountnorris, Sir Richard Phillips, and the author of "My Pocket Book"—Edward Dubois. See account of this publication and of the "Pocket Book" in "The Annual Review," vol. vii. 1808.

C. Forster, of 91, Poultry, published, amongst other works, "The Literary Magazine and British Review," which extended from 1788 to 1794. It is distinguished for a series of well-engraved portraits, mostly by T. Holloway, accompanied by original memoirs; also other prints and essays on literary and scientific subjects.

Under the Royal Exchange, John Richardson, who was a highly respected tradesman, carried on an extensive trade amongst the city merchants. He was one of the original proprietors of "The Beauties of England," and was assisted by a nephew of the same name.

In the same street, Mr. J. Sewell, a worthy but eccentric man, published the "European Magazine;" the biographical articles in which, especially those connected with the drama, were written by Isaac Reed, who edited the work for many years, and was succeeded by Stephen Jones. Mr. Moser was a prolific writer in this popular periodical, which contained many well-engraved portraits. Amongst them was one of Dr. Joseph Priestley, in profile, drawn by myself, from life, when the reverend philosopher was reading a farewell discourse to a crowded congregation in Hackney Church, in March, 1794.

At the northeast corner of Bishopsgate Street, Messrs. Arch, two Quaker brothers, enjoyed an excellent retail trade. They had shares in "The Beauties of England," and were the publishers of Turner and Cooke's "Southern Coast," which contains many fine specimens of the skill of the respective artists. This work, somewhat like "The Beauties," was the cause of repeated disputes between the publishers and the artists and authors. The late amiable William Alexander, then one of the curators of the British Museum, wrote an urgent and kindly-expressed letter to Messrs. Arch, advising them to pay more liberal prices to the engravers. I have a copy of that letter, from the original in possession of Dawson Turner, Esq.

The "Minerva Press," by Wm. Lane, in Leadenhall Street, must not be omitted in this short retrospect of the older metropolitan publishers. It was noted for the number and variety of books, called novels, which were continually produced and distributed to all the circulating libraries in the country. From ten to twenty pounds were the sums usually paid to authors for those novels of three volumes. The Colburns and Bentleys drove this trash out of the market.

Part II.

FLEET STREET, RED LION PASSAGE, CHANCERY LANE, HIGH HOLBORN.

Part II.

FLEET STREET, RED LION PASSAGE, CHANCERY LANE, AND HIGH HOLBORN.

Fleet Street and its Immediate Vicinity—McCreery—Nightingale Rylance—John Major—Walton and Cotton's Angler—Walpole Anecdotes—Rev. T. F. Dibdin—Kearsley—Quarterly Review—John Murray—George Cruikshank—W. Hone and his Trials—Wm. Cobbett—E. Williams—The John Bull—London Magazine and its Contributors—J. Taylor—J. H. Wiffin—Duke of Bedford—T. Bensley—Red Lion Passage—John Nichols and his Literary Anecdotes—A. J. Valpy—Wm. Pickering—The Bridgewater Treatises—High Holborn—The Architectural Antiquities of Great Britain—John Britton's Partners—O. Rees—Josiah Taylor.

FLEET Street and its immediate vicinage are noted in the annals of Literature for the number and estimation of authors, printers, and publishers who have been located here, in addition to those already named. Amongst these may be specified John McCreery, an eminent printer, who had distinguished himself at Liverpool by writing and publishing a poem, called "The Press." This was reprinted and a second part added, on his settling in the metropolis. He was strongly recommended to the London publishers by Mr. Roscoe. In his employ were Ralph Rylance and John Nightingale, two young men, who were afterwards engaged in writing and editing several literary works for London publishers. Three volumes on "London," part of "The Beauties of England," were compiled by the latter, in a very heedless manner. He was author of two octavo volumes, "Portraitures of Methodism" and of "Catholicism." His friend and associate, Rylance, was a learned, diligent, and trustworthy author, and was much employed by the house of Longman and Co. in translations, preparing the manuscripts of inexperienced authors for the press and on miscellaneous literature. He was a most worthy and honourable man. He became deranged in intellect and died in the prime of life, respected by all who knew him.

Benjamin Martin, an optician and author already referred to, had a shop and lived many years in this street. The long list of his publications—more than sixty volumes, all of which were eminently useful, and many of them popular, specified in Watts's "Bibliotheca Britannica"—show that he must have been industrious and scientific; but also prove how fleeting and evanescent is literary fame.

John Major lived on the south side of Fleet Street, for some years, having removed from No. 71, Great Russell Street, Bloomsbury. He was much respected by a numerous circle of book-lovers and book-buyers, and particularly by the followers and disciples of Isaac Walton: by artists, poets, and the friends of the three. A poet, himself, and fond of books, not only as articles to impart good counsel, and the most disinterested and wholesome advice, he was constantly in their company. His shop was well stocked with some of the choicest, and he successively published, with useful and discriminating notation and fine embellishments, "Walton and Cotton on Angling;" the "Physiognomical Portraits," 100 heads beautifully engraved with Biographical Sketches, 2 vols. large 8vo., and large 4to. 1824; "Robinson Crusoe," designs by Stothard; "Hogarth Moralized," by the Rev. Dr. Mavor; Walpole's "Anecdotes of Painting," in 5 vols. imp. 8vo., 1835; "The Cabinet Gallery of Pictures," with Critical Dissertations by Allan Cunningham, 2 vols. imp. 8vo., 1833. This interesting publication contains 72 prints, and a series of essays on the respective subjects and their authors, by one of the most honest and discriminating writers on such matters.

Walpole's "Anecdotes," from the manuscript collections of Virtue, was a work in much estimation by readers in the fine arts, for some time after its publication; but thence to the time Major produced his new edition, there were various sources opened, and further information easily obtainable, for correcting and greatly enlarging the book. Had Major engaged Allan Cunningham instead of the Rev. James Dallaway, he would have benefited himself and have satisfied his critical customers. But, alas! this was not the case: an unsatisfactory and erroneous book was produced, though lavishly embellished with 150 prints of portraits, &c., also good paper and printing. Some of the portraits were skillfully engraved by Robinson, Scriven, Worthington, and Finden. From printing too many copies, a large remainder was sold off after the bankruptcy of its publisher, and Mr. Bohn disposed of them at the reduced prices of £4 for the small, and five guineas the large paper, with India proofs; instead of ten guineas for the former, and fifteen for the latter.

Some of these publications obtained the unqualified encomiums of the Rev. Dr. T. F. Dibdin, in his "Reminiscences of a Literary Life," 1836; but it was unfortunate for the honest bookseller to be too familiar and confiding in the unprincipled parson. The former accepted bills to a large amount drawn by the latter, who failed to honour them, and the consequence was bankruptcy and total ruin. Major sunk never to rise again: for his mind became deranged, and he was placed under restraint. Recovering, in some measure, he was released from the asylum, and found a retreat and comparative comfort in the Charter-house, London, where three other respectable booksellers were then sheltered and maintained in old age.

Mr. Kearsley, of the same street, published the "English Review;" also the "English Encyclopædia," in several quarto volumes: the last publication possessed considerable merit. He also produced many other works, which became exceedingly popular and profitable—the "Beauties" of different authors. Those of Sterne, Johnson, Shakspeare; of the Spectator, Tatler, and Rambler, and other periodicals, were selling for many years, and reprinted in several editions. These, with Adams's "Flowers of Ancient and Modern History," "Flowers of Modern Travels," "English Parnassus," "Curious Thoughts on the History of Man," constituted a large portion of my early library. I have now before me "the eleventh edition" of Sterne's "Beauties," 1790.

In Fleet Street originated "The Quarterly Review," which was commenced in February, 1809, by John Murray. This gentleman, in a respectable line of business, evidently possessed strong religious and political opinions, and was annoyed at the popularity and signal effects which the "Edinburgh Review" was producing in the republic of literature. To oppose, and endeavour to counteract its "virus," as called by Mr. Canning, he addressed a letter to that gentleman,—then Chancellor of the Exchequer,—suggesting and urging the necessity of printing a periodical, the joint production of some of the most eminent Tories of the time, in opposition to the famed "Northern Review." He tells Mr. Canning that "he is no adventurer, but a man of some property, inheriting a business that has been established for nearly a century." This led to a correspondence, and to communications with William Gifford, Walter Scott, George Ellis, Hookham Frere, George Rose, Robert Southey, and some others of name and note, and very speedily to the publication of the first number. The high and rancorous spirit of Tory party, which then prevailed, thus obtained a dauntless champion, who has combated vigorously and intrepidly four times in the year up to the present age of peace, and a comparative truce in the war-fields of politics. Both reviews have produced decided and important effects on the literature and politics of the country; and it cannot fail to interest and instruct the lover of books to look over and compare the early writings in these periodicals with the "Monthly," the "Critical," the "Anti-jacobin," and other "Reviews" which had long occupied the critical market. Mr. Murray removed from Fleet Street to Albemarle Street in 1812, to premises that had been occupied by William Miller, who had published some fine and expensive books. Amongst these were Forster's "British Gallery of Engravings," folio; Blomefield's "History, &c., of Norfolk," 10 vols. 4to. and imp. 8vo.; "The Itinerary of Archbishop Baldwin through Wales," 2 vols. 4to. 1806. The last work is peculiarly impressed on my mind, by a circumstance which gave me much annoyance at the time of its publication. Mr. Miller, knowing that I was acquainted with many book collectors and antiquaries tempted me to subscribe for six copies, by allowing a discount of thirty per cent. under the publishing price, and payment by bill at three months after delivery. This induced me to speculate: I gave the bill, and was prepared to pay on the day it became due. The banker's clerk, however, failed to present it, and on the next day

I had a notice that the bill was at a banker's, and there was 3s. 6d. due for noting the same. Unacquainted with bill transactions, but sensitive to everything that might impeach my credit, I hastened to Albemarle Street and paid the money, explaining that I had remained at home all the preceding day. The clerk's excuse was that Burton Street was too far out of town, and he had not time.

Mr. Murray became popular, successful, and much respected, not only by some of the most talented and eminent authors of his time, but by many of the nobility. His liberality to the literati, his tact in business and general information, were frequently exhibited in his correspondence with the parties above named, and many other distinguished writers. At the social and friendly board, both at home and abroad, he manifested engaging conversational powers; and it has been my good fortune to have been repeatedly amused and informed by him, in company with some of the bright literary planets which have appeared in, but have left, our hemisphere. In my library I often refer to some of those beautiful and valuable books which he has published, and honoured me with as presents.

At No. 55, Fleet Street, William Hone had a

small shop, in 1815, where he published "The Traveller," a newspaper; also "The Life of Elizabeth Fenning," who was hung for attempting to poison an idiot, though Hone's account of her life shows she was guiltless of the act. At this house appeared the first of his famed political pamphlets, which was graphically and effectively illustrated by his young and talented friend, the now eminent literary artist, George Cruikshank. Of this most witty, poignant, morally satiric and talented artist, an interesting biographical essay has been preserved in "The London Journal," November 20th, 1847, from the fluent and discriminating pen of Dr. R. Shelton Mackenzie, with a clever woodcut portrait. This paper not only shows the reader the peculiar graphic merits of the highly-gifted artist, but gives a vivid review of the political and moral character of the age in which he lived and worked, and points out the merits and demerits of some of the most prominent actors on the stage. Hone and Cruikshank continued in association for many years, and had the bookseller fully profited by the counsels of the artist, he might have escaped State prosecutions, become a respectable and successful tradesman, and have lived to witness his friend's pre-eminence. Though they often differed in opinions on religious and even political subjects, they remained in friendly attachment during the chequered life of Hone. I have often wished that the artist had given to the world a graphic and literary review of his own career and connections, and still hope he may be incited to execute it; for his pen and pencil are competent to produce one or two volumes of surpassing and unparalleled interest.

Hone very soon moved from Fleet Street to the Old Bailey, where, in conjunction with Cruikshank, he produced successively and successfully "The Political House that Jack Built," "A Slap at Slop," and three "Parodies on the Book of Common Prayer." The first of these publications became so popular, that more than fifty editions were published, as appears by a volume now before me, entitled "Hone's Popular Political Tracts: containing The House that Jack Built; Queen's Matrimonial Ladder; Right Divine of Kings to Govern Wrong; Political Showman; Man in the Moon; The Queen's Form of Prayer; A Slap at Slop," 8vo. with numerous cuts, for William Hone, 1820. The last pamphlet was a smart and smarting attack on Dr. Stoddart, and his daily paper, called "The New Times." But Hone's Parodies were the most noted, and the most successful in their results, though productive of cruel and vindictive persecution and prosecution to the author. For printing and publishing these, three several indictments for libels were tried against him, in the Court of King's Bench, on the 19th, 20th, and 21st of December, 1817. Justice Abbott presided on the first, and Lord Ellenborough on the second and third days. The strong political prejudices of the latter judge were well known, and became apparent on the trials; but Hone conducted his own defence, with a firmness, fortitude, and talent which astonished both his friends and foes. His addresses to the jury, as stated in a note in the printed report of the trials, lasted, "on the first day, six hours, on the second, seven, and on the third, upwards of eight hours;" yet he was in a bad state of health, oppressed and depressed, and manifested much physical exhaustion. Still he was clear, close, resolute, and self-confident, and was listened to with intense interest by the court, but with evident signs of mortification by the judge. The result was an acquittal upon each indictment. Rarely have there been criminal trials which excited more popular sympathy and curiosity during their progress, or more general rejoicing in their termination. The accused returned to his home in triumph, and a large public subscription was raised on his behalf. He had removed from his small shop in the Old Bailey to a large and expensive house on Ludgate Hill. Here he was followed, caressed, and praised by a succession of visitors— real, or affected friends,—amongst whom were some of the most popular members of opposition in the two Houses. A sum of nearly £4,000 was raised for him by voluntary subscription. With such a vast fortune, to him, and living and faring sumptuously every day, he had neither time nor incentive to write, or attend to shop business. The consequence was natural. The down-hill road from affluence to poverty is often travelled with special-train velocity, and terminates in the "slough of despond." Such was the case with our once-fortunate, but many times unfortunate, political and poetical hero; for a short time his affairs were involved in the labyrinth of bankruptcy; and ruin, irretrieveable ruin, ensued, from which he never became released. In February, 1834, he appealed to the Literary Fund for aid, when he intreated my intercession in his behalf, in a letter, wherein he says: "I am too much enfeebled to move about, and my family is in great distress, and I am worried out by little claims upon me, and have not a shilling." The Committee of that noble institution inquired into his case and character, and finding the first to be urgent, and the second to be more "sinned against than sinning," awarded him a handsome grant. I knew him well, and respected him for warmth of heart, kindness of disposition, and strength of head; but he was most improvident and indiscreet in the management of money affairs. Had these been placed in the charge of an honest, good accountant, William Hone might have lived to be a rich man, and died a happy one. His later publications were useful and valuable, as calculated to combine amusing with good historical, topographical, and antiquarian information. They were "The Every-Day Book," "The Year Book," "The Table Book," and "Ancient Mysteries." Never, perhaps, was political and personal satire, irony, ridicule, burlesque, caricature, sarcasm, and unflinching temerity of language and graphic representation carried to such a pitch as in his once-popular pamphlets, which, with the exalted and illustrious personages represented and ridiculed, are now scarcely to be descried in the haze of distance. Had there not been gross delinquency and bad conduct in the parties satirized, and also palpable originality and talent in the author and the artist, these publications would not have attained their surprising and unprecedented popularity.

The Poets' Gallery, 192, Fleet Street, was a place of much distinction at the end of the last century and beginning of the present. Thomas Macklin, its proprietor, was a publisher and print-seller, and besides using the Gallery for temporary exhibitions, continued to keep on view a succession of works of art; amongst which was the popular picture of "The Woodman," by Thomas Barker, of Bath. Many of these were painted by the most eminent English artists for the splendid "Bible," which he published. This was produced in rivalry of Boydell's magnificent "Shakspeare" and Bowyer's "England." These contemporary publications surpassed all literary works either of this or any other country; as comprising and displaying the finest examples of paper and typography, with the highest specimens of the fine arts of England. Herein Bowyer, Boydell, and Macklin did more to benefit art, and the sciences connected with printing, than had ever before been done, or perhaps will be effected, by any triumvirate of tradesmen. Macklin died at the early age of 43, in Oct. 1800. The Gallery has since been occupied as an auction-room.

The old-established bookselling firm of Benjamin and John White, at No. 63, Fleet Street, was amongst the most respectable of the class in London fifty years ago. Its stock was large and of the best books. They published some fine works in Natural History; amongst which were those of Pennant, Latham, and White, of Selborne. The last was a relation to the booksellers, as acknowledged by John, who edited the collected edition of his works in 2 vols. 8vo. 1802, in which is a very brief notice of that most amusing and amiable author. The last of the Whites of Fleet Street joined in partnership with J. G. Cochrane.

The once-noted and eminently-notorious William Cobbett issued many of his remarkable "Weekly Registers" from an office in this street, and, for several years afterwards, from his printing establishment in Bolt Court, where most of his voluminous publications on history, politics, travels, grammar, &c., were produced. In the annals of the human race, and particularly amongst its remarkable men, Cobbett appears conspicuous, if not pre-eminent. Emerging from the humblest of peasant society, without education, and struggling against many difficulties and privations, he advanced himself to high political and national distinction, obtaining a seat in the British Parliament, and writing several volumes, which secured great celebrity for some years, and which will be read with surprise and gratification in future ages. His works are numerous, very voluminous, and on various subjects. Amongst them is a copious, and apparently very candid Auto-Biography, which details a pretty faithful account of his public career and writings. But I would more particularly direct the young reader to "The Life of William Cobbett," a small thick volume in 18mo., of which the third edition appeared in 1835, extending to 422 pages. This is dedicated "To the Sons of William Cobbett," and contains apparently a fair, discriminating account of the man, the author, and the politician. It also reprints the opinions and criticisms of Wm. Hazlitt, Gifford in the "Standard," and others from the "Morning Chronicle," the "Times," and the "Atlas." Charles Knight has recorded his opinions and remarks on Cobbett, in the "History of England during the Thirty Years' Peace," vol. i. p. 48.

At 186, Fleet Street, was the shop of the Eton School Books, for many years conducted by Edward Williams, grandson of Joseph Pote, the historian of Windsor. He was one of the Court Assistants of the Stationers' Company for the last five or six years of his life, and proved himself an active and zealous member of that famed corporation. He was also active in the committee of the Literary Fund, and there, as well as in public and private life, manifested general benevolence, suavity of manners, true philanthropy, and those social, amiable traits of disposition, which conciliate all associates. Hence his company was generally courted. To a natural cheerfulness of temper he added the happy qualification of writing and singing songs, appropriate to times, persons, and places. In Jan. 1838, as he was walking in one of the streets of London, near the Haymarket, he fell on an ice slide, and received such serious injury as occasioned his speedy death. His eldest son, Edward Pote Williams, has succeeded him both in London and at Eton.

"The John Bull," weekly newspaper, has been printed and published at No. 40 Fleet Street, ever since its commencement in Dec. 1820. If not projected and edited at first by the celebrated Theodore Hook, it is generally known that he was intimately connected with it for many years, and that he wrote many of its highly poignant articles. Conservative and of high church principles, it has continued an unflinching course of advocating these two branches of the government, and to censure and ridicule all classes of society, and all departments of politicians of opposite opinions. The eminently witty, and as eminently reckless, editor soon rendered it popular and profitable to the proprietors, and to himself, by the severity of its political articles, and by the poignant wit and satire of its personal and literary essays. It is said that he derived at least £2000 a year from writings in this journal; at the same time he was in receipt of nearly as much more for novels, farces, &c.: yet he was often in debt and embarrassment. Never, perhaps, was there a man of such precocious and versatile talents. "As a wit, confessed without rival to shine," his company was courted, and he was incessantly flattered by princes, nobles, and the most noted in the world of fashion and of fame. As a writer of novels, farces, songs, and particularly in improvisation, he was, perhaps, unrivalled in the world of genius. Having been several times in his fascinating company, I can bear witness to these qualifications: when in contact and competition with the famed authors of "The Rejected Addresses," he seemed to shine with additional brilliancy. Yet this man, this accomplished wit and novelist, was imprisoned and degraded for disreputable neglect of his duties in a public government office, in which he was misplaced by political friends. His story and his leading characteristics are well described in the last volume of Knight's "Penny Cyclopædia."

"The Dispatch," of 139, Fleet Street, a weekly

newspaper diametrically opposed to the "John Bull," has continued to have a popular and prosperous career from 1818 to the present time. Besides a copious amount of political matter and general news, this journal has long been noted for its smart reviews of literary works, the fine arts, the drama, and the theatres. For some years my respected friend, Edward Dubois, contributed numerous witty articles on those subjects.

At No. 93 in this street, "The London Magazine" was published, by Taylor and Hessey, from Midsummer 1821 to the same month in 1825. It was edited by Mr. Taylor, who made the work highly popular, with the aid of such men as Henry Southern (now our Ambassador at Brazil), J. H. Reynolds, Thos. Hood, Chas. Lamb, the Rev. H. F. Cary, Allan Cunningham, Barry Cornwall, Charles Phillips, Horace Smith, Charles A. Elton, Thomas De Quincy, Wm. Hazlitt, Bernard Barton, J. Clare, the Rev. G. Croly, Hartley Coleridge, Dr. Bowring, Thomas Carlyle, and other similar writers. With such a phalanx of wits and literati (now nearly all dead), it is not surprising that this periodical was very popular. In 1827, these publishers sold the magazine to a new editor and proprietor. They published some works of older and eminent authors, under careful editorial superintendence, and embellished from clever designs by Hilton, who was then coming into notice, and who attained just honours as an artist of the higher class. Taylor and Hessey brought out several successful books by the amiable moral writers, Mrs. and Miss Jane Taylor, of Ongar (no relatives of the publisher), and also other works. They afterwards removed to Waterloo Place, and on the establishment of the London University, Mr. Taylor was appointed its bookseller, which induced him to settle in Upper Gower Street, where he has continued in co-operation with Mr. Walton to the present time. He is author of a well-written volume on the controverted and never-ending dispute as to the authorship of Junius's Letters, in which he endeavours to prove that Sir Philip Francis was the writer; but of which evidence I cannot admit the validity. In a learned volume, "The Emphatic New Testament," and other works on scriptural criticism, and in several pamphlets on currency, Mr. Taylor displays much erudition and acute logical argument.

Arthur Collins, called by Watt ("Bib. Brit.") "the laborious antiquary and heraldic writer," who was editor and publisher, if not author, of the first edition of the English Peerage, in 1700, then lived at the Black Boy, in Fleet Street. Edward Curll published several books "at the Dial and Bible, St. Dunstan's Church." Bernard Lintot was living here at the beginning of the last century; and the amiable Izaak Walton was a denizen of this district. The first edition of his "Angler" was published in 1653, in St. Dunstan's Churchyard, price 1s. 6d.—(A copy sold at Haworth's sale for thirteen guineas.)

Michael Drayton, the poet, died in a house near Saint Dunstan's Church, according to Aubrey. The same authority tells us that Cowley, the more voluminous author, was the son of a grocer in this street. T. Snelling, who drew, engraved, and published numerous plates on English Coins, had a shop in this street, where he dealt in those, in medals, &c.

Branching off from Fleet Street, to the south, is Bouverie Street, at the bottom of which my once much-esteemed and confidential friend, James Moyes, built large premises for a printing establishment, after the destruction, by fire, of his former offices in Greville Street. Here he produced numerous literary works for different publishers, also some for private friends, and was in an extended and respectable way of business, when the severe commercial panic of 1826 involved him, with several of his friends, in bankruptcy. The shock was much more severe to his susceptible nerves, and high sense of honor, than the former calamity. His mental and corporeal faculties seemed paralyzed for some weeks, and his friends were alarmed; but rallying, and aided by a few gentlemen who knew his integrity of principle and moral worth, he took new premises in Castle Street, Leicester Square, where he progressively obtained a large amount of business, and was prosperous and happy, until death arrested his career in 1838, at the age of 59. He was interred in a vault in the cemetery of Kensal Green, where a marble slab is placed to his memory. Intimately acquainted with this honourable tradesman for a quarter of a century, I can conscientiously assert that he fully deserved the encomium Pope applies to "the noblest work of God"—an honest man. I never knew a person more widely and uniformly esteemed. In business, he actively and zealously endeavoured to secure the confidence and good opinion of every employer; and, I believe, was always successful. As a man, he was well informed, upright, kind-hearted ,and generous both in word and deed, and as completely exempt from the infirmities of poor human nature as any of his species. With such qualities, and a thorough knowledge of business, he must have attained a good fortune in a few years.

He printed different literary works for me, entirely to my satisfaction and to his own credit. Besides being employed by many respectable publishers, he printed "The Literary Gazette" and "Fraser's Magazine" for many years; also several successive volumes of "The Gems of Beauty," "Friendship's Offering," and other works, under the editorship of Lady Blessington. He also worked for the "Admiralty" and for other public offices; and produced two handsome and beautifully printed books for J. H. Wiffin, of "Jerusalem Delivered," and "Historical Memoirs of the House of Russell," in two vols. royal octavo. This led to a connection with John, Duke of Bedford, for whom Mr. Moyes printed different works, on the pictures, statues, grasses, ferns, &c., at Woburn Abbey. I have now before me letters from this truly generous nobleman, also from Lady Blessington, Mr. Wiffin, and others, expressing approbation of his works, and thanking him for skill and kind attentions. Though I have been acquainted with several Quakers, I never met with one who was more sincere, candid, warm-hearted, and unsophisticated than Mr. Wiffin. He united with these qualifications the susceptibility of the poet with the perseverance and discrimination of the faithful historian. His "Memoirs of the House of Russell," which were printed by Mr. Moyes in 1832, will justify these remarks, and will derive further confirmation by his translation of Tasso's "Jerusalem Delivered," with a series of beautifully-executed engravings in wood, also in two smaller volumes. He produced a volume of Miscellaneous Poems, under the title of "Aonian Hours," and other poetry. Mr. Wiffin was Librarian to John, Duke of Bedford, in which honourable office he died, in May 1836, in the prime of life, much beloved by all who knew him. A well-written account of his personal and literary character is preserved in the "Literary Gazette," May 1836. He has been succeeded by John Martin, formerly in partnership with Mr. Rodwell, of Bond Street, and who, in 1834, published "A Bibliographical Catalogue of Privately-printed Books," a handsome and curious volume.

In Bolt Court was the printing-office of Thomas Bensley, which attained marked distinction at the end of the last century and beginning of the present. It was here that Mr. Konig's printing machinery was first employed, and advanced towards perfection; and from this office issued, in 1797, a magnificent royal folio edition of Thomson's "Seasons." Here also were printed Macklin's Bible and many other fine books; likewise my (Britton's) fourth volume of "Architectural Antiquities," and the "History of Redcliffe Church." These premises, like too many other printing-offices of London, suffered by fire: first, on the fifth of November, 1807, when they were much damaged, with several works, by a fire supposed to have been occasioned by careless boys. Again, June 1819, the whole, with their valuable contents, were consumed in or materially injured by another conflagration.

"Red Lion Passage," at the end of the last century and beginning of the present, was familiar to a large class of readers of the "Gentleman's Magazine," and to every topographer and antiquary in England, by the spacious printing-office of John Nichols; and the many publications issuing therefrom. This veteran, respectable, and truly valuable periodical ("Gentleman's Magazine") has continued its monthly course from 1731 to the present time; and it is a singular part of its history that it was commenced by a journeyman printer, and for ninety-six years was continued under the editorship of three. In accordance with the spirit of the times, this venerable journal has now all the freshness, vigour, beauty and interest, which good writing, paper, and typography can impart. I was indulged by my venerated and kind friend, the "Deputy of Farringdon Ward," with the use of any books in his valuable topographical library, but none were to be taken away; for he justly remarked, these were his working-tools almost in daily demand. I found them invaluable to me at a time when my own stock was very small—when the reading-room of the British Museum was not easily accessible, and when I had engaged to write and print "The Beauties of Wiltshire;" and also, in conjunction with my literary coadjutor, Mr. Brayley, "Topographical Accounts of Bedfordshire, Berkshire, and Buckinghamshire," for the first volume of "The Beauties of England." This courtesy, however, proved of great benefit, as was also the personal intercourse and converse with the author of the "History of Leicestershire," in eight folio volumes, his valuable "Literary Anecdotes," in nine volumes, with two of indexes, and of other similar works. Here I occasionally saw Richard Gough, who was a frequent visitor; and here I also had glances of other eminent topographers and antiquaries, who employed the same respected printer and author. Some years afterwards, I was honoured and gratified by friendly intimacy with most of the personages to whom I then looked up with awful respect and admiration. They are all removed from this terrestrial sphere, but have left their names, and varied qualifications, indelibly recorded in the lasting pages of their respective publications. With Mr. Nichols, I continued on friendly terms from the end of the last century to the time of his death, Nov. 26, 1826. By a fall in Red Lion Passage, in January 1807, he fractured a thigh-bone, by which he was lamed for life; and in February of the following year he suffered severely from a calamitous fire, which destroyed his premises, and a large stock of paper, printed books, manuscripts, &c. At the time of my early communion with Mr. Nichols, his son John Bowyer, was taken into partnership, and continued so for nearly a quarter of a century. In such an office and its associations, it is not surprising that he became an antiquary and topographer as well as printer; and that his son, John Gough, should be one of the mose devoted, zealous, and learned amongst the present numerous class of archæologists.

A. J. Valpy, M.A., a son of the learned Dr. Valpy, of Reading School, after being a short time in Tooke's Court, removed to the more spacious offices vacated by Mr. Nichols, in which he executed, besides many other works, "The Delphin Classics," with the Variorum Notes. These extended to 141 volumes, which were charged 18s.

each, and in large paper, £1. 16s. He also printed, for different publishers, many other books, both in Greek and Latin, and not only employed some of the most learned compositors that could be obtained, but several scholars from the Universities, to read and correct the proof-sheets. Hence the Valpy office and press obtained high distinction in the learned world. Mr. Valpy retired from business in the prime of life, to enjoy "otium cum dignitate."

Nearly opposite to the printing-office last referred to was a small house occupied by Stephen Jones, a gentleman with whom I was on familiar terms for many years. He was Secretary to a Freemasons' lodge, and was occasionally employed by some of the publishers to edit and arrange miscellaneous papers, make indexes, &c. He first appeared, in 1791, as abridging Burke's "Reflections;" and two years afterwards his name was attached to an Abridgment of Ward's "Natural History," in 3 vols. In 1796 he produced "A Biographical Dictionary in Miniature," a copy of which he presented me, with his autograph: the first literary work I had then received, though I can now enumerate more than sixty volumes. He produced several other publications, which are specified in Watt's "Bibliotheca Britannica," the last of which is "A Pronouncing Dictionary of the English Language," a large octavo volume. The third edition of the work, now before me, has the author's autograph, with the date of 1798. He also edited a new edition of the "Biographia Dramatica:" this was harshly criticised, when he published a pamphlet, entitled "Hypercriticism Exposed, in a Letter to the Readers of the Quarterly Review," 8vo. 1812.

Towards the end of his life, my respected friend, a man of mild disposition, strict honesty, great industry, and unblemished character, was embarrassed in circumstances, applied to, and derived pecuniary aid from, the Literary Fund. Dr. N. Drake, in a letter to Cadell and Davies, respecting his large work, "Shakspeare and His Times," says, "S. Jones was the compositor to my Essays on Periodical Literature, and I was perfectly satisfied with his accuracy and attention;" whence he strongly recommended him to those publishers to make the index to his two quarto volumes. It extends to six quarto sheets.

In New Street and New Street Square are the large and famed printing-offices of Strahan, "the King's Printer," who obtained great wealth, and at whose presses an immense number of books have been printed. Among these was the "Cyclopædia," edited by my early and much-loved friend, Dr. A. Rees, and for which I wrote many a colsely-packed page. Besides accounts of nearly all the cities, towns, and counties of England, Wales, and Scotland, I wrote separate articles on Avebury and Stonehenge, with illustrative prints, and a memoir of Shakspeare. With copy and proofs I had frequent communication with one of the offices, for there were several, and witnessed the order, discipline, and admirable system which prevailed. The liberality and riches of Andrew Strahan, Esq., who died in August 1831, render his name illustrious in the annals of man. In 1822, he presented £1000 to the Literary Fund, and bequeathed a similar sum after his decease, in the year 1831. He also gave other large sums to different charitable societies. He died, in the 83rd year of his age, at the house in New Street, leaving property to the amount of above one million of money; and presented his great printing establishment to his nephew, Andrew Spottiswoode, who married one of the daughters of Mr. T. N. Longman, of Paternoster Row.

In Chancery Lane, north of Fleet Street, was a shop which William Pickering gave name and note to by publishing many valuable volumes under the titles of "Aldine Edition of the Poets;"

"Walton and Cotton's Angler," and other books on the subject; Richardson's Dictionaries of the English Language; Greek, Latin, Italian, and Diamond Classics; and several works on Ecclesiastical, Biblical, and Polemical History; on Anglo-Saxon and Anglo-Norman Literature; "Small Books on Great Subjects, by Well-Wishers to Knowledge;" and last, though not least in merit and popularity, the novel, unique, and original "Bridgewater Treatises," in 12 volumes. These were by Sir Charles Bell, on the "Hand;" the Rev. William Buckland, D.D., on "Geology and Mineralogy;" the Rev. Thomas Chalmers, D.D., on the "Moral and Intellectual Constitution of Man;" John Kidd, M. D., on the "Physical Condition of Man;" the Rev. William Kirby, on the "History, Habits, and Instincts of Animals;" William Prout, M. D., on "Chemistry, Meteorology, and the Function of Digestion;" P. M. Roget, M. D., on "Animal and Vegetable Physiology;" and the Rev. W. Whewell, on "Astronomy and General Physics."

These Essays were written by the respective learned authors, in compliance with a bequest of Francis Henry, Earl of Bridgewater, in February 1829, of £8000. to be paid for eight Treatises "On the Power, Wisdom, and Goodness of God, as manifested in the Creation." Never, perhaps, in the annals of the human race, and of testamentary generosity and rightful application, was a legacy more wisely and laudably given. It was Mr. Pickering's good fortune to be selected as the publisher of the series, whence his house and character were prominently brought under the notice of the reading world. In 1843 he removed to 177, Piccadilly, where may be seen a house full of rare and valuable books, and where may be obtained many of those he had printed and published, under the editorial care, learning, and ability of Sir Harris Nicolas, Basil Montagu, the Rev. W. L. Bowles, S. W. Singer, the Rev. Alexander Dyce, the Rev. J. Mitford, J. H. Marsden, Thomas Wright, Robert Roscoe, George Daniel, W. Tooke, the Rev. Dr. T. F. Dibdin, and many other authors of eminence.

Let us look at a "Pen and Ink Sketch" of Mr. Pickering by the last-named reverend gentleman, in his own peculiar style of touch and effect. "How does Mr. Pickering this morning? and where are the Caxtons, and Wynkyns, and Pynsons—his Alduses, Elzevirs, and Michel Le Noirs? But Mr. Pickering has a note of louder triumph to sound, in being publisher of the 'Bridgewater Treatises,' which bid fair to traverse the whole civilized portion of the globe."—(Reminiscences, p. 904.)

From Chancery Lane to High Holborn is a mere step, and there, at No. 59, is a house, which was built by Josiah Taylor, the Architectural Bookseller, with whom I (Britton) became acquainted at the early part of my literary career, and with whom I fortunately continued on intimate terms to the time of his lamented death, January, 1834. In 1805, I showed him some drawings of ancient buildings which Mr. Hood thought were not calculated to adorn the pages, and come under the title, of "The Beauties of England." After a little consultation and deliberation, it was agreed to publish a new quarto work, entitled "The Architectural Antiquities of Great Britain." A plan was digested, a prospectus was written, Longman and Co. engaged to take a third share in the work, and be the publishers. Hence originated a publication, which not only extended to five quarto volumes, and brought before the public 360 engravings, representing a great variety of old buildings of the country, but many of historical, descriptive, and critical essays. These were not by my own pen only, but by those of several gentlemen, who thus laid before the reading world much original and interesting information. This work, indeed, gave origin to a new school of artists, both draftsmen and engravers, and to many competing and rival publications. It obtained great popularity, and was consequently profitable to the publishers and to the author. Had the latter been a little more the man of business, and more anxious to obtain wealth than fame, he might have been enabled to retire from the labours and anxieties of authorship at the age of eighty, with competence to provide all the comforts, and even some of the luxuries of life. His chief solicitude and ambition, throughtout the whole extent of that and other publications, have been to render them truthful, original, correct, and replete with the best artistic illustrations and literary information which he could obtain and impart to the reader. His partners were confiding and kind, upon most occasions; and Mr. Taylor evinced his friendship by a posthumous bequest. Mr. O. Rees proved himself a warm and even affectionate friend throughout life.

Mr. Taylor was a punctilious, preservering, and honourable man of business, and confined his attention, and publications almost exclusively to those devoted to architecture and engineering. Hence he became acquainted with most of the professional gentlemen of the kingdom, published for many of them, and was connected in business with nearly all. Thus we find that his catalogue of works contains the following amongst other names: Stuart and Revett, Soane, Malton, G. Richardson, Peter Nicholson, Lugars, Gwilt, Pocock, Dearn, Gandy, Aikin, Plaw; and the following on "Gothic Architecture," the Rev. G. D. Whittington, the Rev. J. Milner, the Rev. James Dallaway, the Rev. Joseph Warton, James Bentham, Captain Grose, the Rev. J. Gunn, the Rev. George Millers, and J. S. Hawkins. The Essays, by Milner, Warton, Bentham, and Grose, were published by Mr. Taylor in a separate volume, which went through three editions.

Towards the latter part of his life he purchased a good house at Stockwell, where he was in the habit of assembling frequently a succession of friends around his social board; and there I have often met, and enjoyed the converse of, some of the most eminent architects and engineers of London. On those occasions it was his practice to send a carriage to and from London to convey two, three, or four gentlemen who did not keep carriages. In the year 1822 the house and shop, in Holborn, with their contents, were consumed by an accidental fire, whereby I sustained a considerable loss. Mr. Taylor died at the age of 73, in the year 1834, and was buried in Bunhill Fields cemetery.

LITERARY LONDON.

"Readings and Music" were popular sources of amusement in London, about fifty years back; and I not only exhibited myself at the place described, but at a large room in Foster Lane, in another at the Globe, Fleet Street, and, lastly, in two others at the Freemasons' Hall, and in the Argyle Rooms. These societies assumed pompous Greek names—"Museodeans," and "Odechorologeans,"—with parade and much etiquette, in aping the operatic customs and manners of theatric and ball-room concerts. The large rooms at both places were crowded with company, every night of performing; and amongst the performers were Miss Brunton, Miss F. Kelly, Miss S. Booth, Miss Bolton, &c.

Part III.

THE STRAND, PALL MALL, KING STREET.

Part III.

THE STRAND, PALL MALL, KING STREET.

The Strand at the beginning of the Century—Thomas Caddell—The Newspaper Press—George Lane—D. Stuart—John Bell—Rudolph Ackermann and his publications—F. Shoberl, Author and Editor—Annuals—,,Dr. Syntax"—Combe—Rowlandson—John and Leigh Hunt—The Literary Gazette—Richardson's Auctions—Geographers—Prince Sanders — Lyceum Theatre—Auctioneers—The Sothebys—Evans—The Christies' Sale-Rooms—Pall Mall—King Street—Covent Garden—Hogarth's Election — P. Luckombe—King and Lochee's Auction Rooms ; their book-sales.

THE STRAND, at the end of the last century and beginning of the present, when a much narrower street than it is now, and when Exeter 'Change occupied a large area of the road-way between the present Lyceum Theatre and Exeter Street, contained several booksellers and publishers of distinction. Amongst these was the house of Alderman Thomas Cadell, which occupied the site of old Jacob Tonson's (the Shakspeare Head).

Andrew Miller, a friend of Thomson, Fielding, Hume, Robertson, was the master of Alderman Cadell.

At the period to which my notes chiefly relate, Alderman Thomas Cadell was living in the Strand, and I had the pleasure of being occasionally in his society. He resigned the business to his Son and to William Davies, jointly, who long traded under the well-known firm of "Cadell and Davies." The Alderman was accustomed to say that he was chiefly indebted for his prosperity to the works of four "Bees,' alluding to four popular publications: "Blair's Sermons," "Blackstone's Commentaries," "Burn's Justice of the Peace," and "Buchan's Domestic Medicine." Johnson's "Dictionary," and Hume and Smollett's "History of England," were also amongst the valuable copyrights belonging to this firm. In reference to the two publications last-mentioned, this establishment, in conjunction with Longman and Co., who were part proprietors with them in those and other works, had to encounter a vigorous opposition from other booksellers when the copyrights expired; but their operations were so judiciously and promptly conducted that they effectually maintained their ground. The "Dictionary" had been published in two costly volumes, folio; and when the copyright was about to expire, an edition in one folio volume was prepared, with great secrecy, by a bookseller in Paternoster Row. The proprietors of the book hearing of that scheme, prepared an edition in two quarto volumes, which, being of a more commodious form, at once became a popular work, and obtained a rapid sale: whereas the rival undertaking involved the speculator in a serious loss. The quarto edition, being published at £5. 5s., produced a considerable profit to the shareholders, who were proportionably tenacious of maintaining its integrity. One of them, however, the managing partner, happening to say vauntingly in the presence of Mr. Childs, an energetic printer at Bungay, that the partners would ruin any one who set up a rival edition, he forthwith stereotyped and reprinted the entire work in a single volume, imperial 8vo. (now currently sold for 18s.) and employing that indefatigable and unscrupulous agent, the late John Ogle Robinson, (formerly of the firm Robinson, Hurst, and Co.) a large and remunerative sale was speedily obtained, and the quarto was consequently much depreciated.

The standard octavo edition of the "History of England" was issued by Cadell and the Longmans, in anticipation of opposition, in periodical numbers, embellished with portraits. Both Cooke and Parsons, nevertheless, entertained the project of duodecimo editions, without prints; but the proprietors forestalled them by a similar edition, with reduced copies of the engravings. The rival publishers proceeded, however, with their respective undertakings, and so great was the sale of the works, that each edition reimbursed its expenses. By a volume of "Autograph Letters and Papers," one of a series now before me, belonging to my friend, Mr. John Wodderspoon, I find that the above-named firm embarked a large capital, at great risk, on Dr. Drake's "Shakspeare and his Times;"Lyson's "Magna Britannica," and Samuels's "Britannia Romana;" G. Chalmers's "Caledonia;" Alexander Chalmers's "British Poets," 21 vols. royal 8vo.; Coxe's Works, (mostly written by Henry Hatcher) Dr. Clarke's Travels, and several other expensive publications. By memoranda amongst this correspondence, it is also evident that they acted with much courtesy and liberality to those authors. Dr. Drake was paid £800 for his two volumes; and in a statement of accounts it seems that the losses were above £900. The works by the Lysonses entailed a great loss on the respectable publishers. Hence we learn that, after their decease, a large stock of unsold books came into the market, and were dispersed at very low prices.

Near the middle part of the ever-crowded, noisy, tumultuous thoroughfare called the Strand, is the very focus—the hot-bed, the forcing-house—of the "Newspaper-Press," now emphatically called "The Fourth Estate." This literary manufactory and news-mart may be almost regarded as exemplifying the perpetual motion. From dawn to night, and thence to dawn again, here is a continued, never-ceasing succession of editors and sub-editors, reporters of various topics, correspondents from foreign states, and from the provinces, merchants and manufacturers, politicians and players, compositors, pressmen, and engineers; also crowds of news-vendors and letter-carriers, with carts and horses to convey loads of wet Papers to railway stations. Could an inquiring and acute foreigner see and appreciate the whole working of this complicated machine, he would marvel, and vainly attempt to give a full and vivid account of it to his distant friends and countrymen. During the sitting of Parliament, and when warmly-contested party questions are under discussion, the activity and excitement in this region are only to be compared to a hive of bees, at the time of swarming. Unlike the generality of London business, that of the News-press is generally conducted during the night, and whilst most people are reposing in bed. Hence we see the windows of the offices fully lighted up, and hear the continued rattle and noise of steam machines and presses in ceaseless operation. I cannot reflect on the comparative and contrasted state of the Newspaper-press, in its mechanical and literary characteristics, as it was at the beginning of the century, when I was occasionally admitted into the editor's "sanctum," and as it is now, when such important reforms have been produced in all departments of paper, type, ink, and particularly in machinery; but still more in the independence and integrity, the vigour and comprehensiveness of editorial writings, without feeling astonished and delighted. It is these improvements and powers which have conspired to gain for the English Press the political title above-named. To the late James Perry, John Walter, Thomas Barnes, and a few other talented and honest men, much of these effects are to be ascribed; and I indulge the hope that others of like powers may continue in the same ranks, and act as substantial checks against every species of tyranny and dishonesty in church and state, in law and commerce, and, indeed, in all gradations of civilized society.

At No. 15, back of St. Clement's, Strand, "The British Press" and "The Globe" first made their public appearance in 1803, "with new and high pretensions," and were ostensibly started by, and intended to promote the views and trading speculations of, the publishing booksellers. These had justly complained of the capricious charges made by the Newspaper proprietors for advertisements, and also for the heedless manner in which notices of fine and expensive literary publications were associated with vile and disgusting quack puffs. To remedy such evils, and obtain a medium between themselves and the public, they procured premises, type, an editor, and the combined establishment for conducting a newspaper. George Lane was engaged as editor, who had been on the "Morning Post," and the "Courier," under Daniel Stuart. This gentleman wrote an explanation of the dispute between the publishers and newspaper proprietors in the "Gentleman's Magazine" (Sept. 1838) to vindicate himself and his brothers of the periodical press, and impeach the former. Mr. George Lane, in the same magazine, published a reply and justification of the booksellers. Among the reforms and improvements which the present denizens of London have cause to rejoice in, when compared with their predecessors, who lived amidst and under numerous annoyances of savage warfare, may be specified the relief from ruthless gangs of street news-vendors, who infested the peaceable and nervous inhabitants with noises that surpassed bedlamites broke loose. Tin horns, of different calibre and sounds, mixed with yells and bawling of men and boys, in troops, who paraded the quiet streets proclaiming, "News! Great news! Bloody news! Armies slaughtered by thousands and tens of thousands:—'Currior'! Extraordinary 'Currior'!! Sixth edition of 'The Currior'!!! &c., &c."

By examining some early numbers of the "British Press," I cannot wonder that it failed to secure purchasers, and consequently did not answer the requirements of the speculators. Poor paper, bad printing, tasteless display, and inefficiency of editorship, are conspicuous. Mr. Lane acknowledged that "the actual sale did not exceed two hundred." The "British Press" proved a complete failure, and it was given up. The "Globe" was, however, continued, under new proprietary management, and is still among the diurnal journals.

John Bell, of the Strand.—Not only as an enterprising and spirited publisher, but as an author, this gentleman continued before the public many years, and brought forward a succession of literary and embellished works which gratified and gave profitable employ to numerous writers, artists, printers, stationers, &c. His "British Poets," "British Theatre," part of which includes the plays of Shakspeare; his "Weekly Messenger," commenced May,. 1796; the "New Weekly Messenger," a paper of unprecedented quantity and varied literary matter, commenced in 1832; his "New Pantheon, or Historical Dictionary of Heathen Gods, Demi-Gods, Goddesses, &c.," which Lowndes calls "an excellent and useful compilation;" and his "Classical Arrangement of Fugitive Poetry," in 18 vols., were each and all variously popular, and calculated to gratify and improve the minds and taste of readers by their literary and graphic contents. In embellishments, he employed the best artists of the age, both for designs and for engravings. He also produced a monthly periodical called "La Belle Assemblée."

Rudolph Ackermann, from Germany, settled in the Strand, opposite old Exeter 'Change, at the latter part of the last century, as a Printseller; and by perseverance, industry, and skill in business, with some knowledge of art, progressively advanced himself and his establishment to the highest degree of prosperity and credit. When I first became acquainted with him, in 1800, his shop was small, and his first floor was let to my friend, George Holmes, an artist, who was induced by my suggestion to publish, in 1801, an octavo volume, "Sketches of a Tour through the South Part of Ireland.' The artist, though possessed of abilities and of very engaging manners, did not advance in life so fast as his landlord, who soon required and occupied the whole house, and increased his business, family, and fortune. He then moved to larger premises, at No. 101, Strand, which occupied part of the site of the old Fountain Tavern, celebrated in the days of Steele, Addison, Pope, &c. Here was also a famed drawing academy, in which Richard Cosway, F. Wheatley, Shipley, and others, afterwards men of fame, were pupils. The more noted lecture-room of John Thelwall present large and commodious "Repository," at the corner of Beaufort Buildings, from the designs of Mr. Papworth. This building occupies the site of five previous houses. The new edifice was provided with a fine and spacious gallery, at the rear, in which were constantly on view a vast number and variety of works of art. The architect also made many designs, and wrote essays for Ackermann's Magazine. The shop, the staircase, the gallery, &c., were not only lighted but brilliantly illuminated by night, with gas, which was manufactured on the premises, from apparatus which Mr. Ackermann had invented, and which was supplied with Canal, or Kennel coal, producing the most vivid light. During the first winter, after these works were completed, crowds of the nobility, gentry, and artists, were in the habit of visiting the place every night, to see the splendid novelties. Once a week the proprietor opened his galleries for a Soirée, where I often met many of the most eminent artists and men of science of our own and of foreign countries. Amongst numerous interesting articles displayed on these occasions was a copy of the spirited proprietor's work on Westminster Abbey, printed on vellum and bound in two large volumes; one containing the letter-press, printed in Bensley's best manner, the other comprising proofs of the plates and the original drawings, also skilfully mounted. The binding, of the most sumptuous kind, alone cost Mr. Ackermann nearly three hundred pounds! This very splendid work is now in the possession of John Allnut, Esq., of Clapham, whose gallery of pictures by English Artists not only reflects honour on his taste and liberality, but on his patriotism.

This article alone serves to give some notion

of the liberal and enterprising disposition of the amiable and estimable German, who manifested a corresponding liberality and enthusiasm in all his business speculations and intercourse with artists and literati. Mr. Shoberl tells me that he paid William Combe at least £400. a year for many successive years, and that he was often a guest at his table; that he proved a friend to him during his last illness, and not only contributed towards, but waited on several of his rich friends to solicit aid in the expenses for the funeral, tomb, &c.

To this improvident, indiscreet man, to T. Rowlandson, to W. H. Pyne, and to several other persons, he was the warm and generous patron. Indeed in all his public dealings, as well as in private life, he displayed generosity, courtesy, frankness, sincerity, and unostentatious benevolence. After the disastrous, murderous, and devasting wars of the French Revolution, the Germans were reduced to the most distressing condition. Poverty and privation pervaded their towns, their villages, and their entire provinces. The English, as usual, afforded many of the emigrants homes and sustenance. To Mr. Ackermann they were indebted for a vast amount of aid and comfort. He took a most active and zealous part in obtaining subscriptions and remitting money to his countrymen. No less than £250,000. were collected for the sufferers in Great Britain, £100,000. of which were voted by Parliament; and as a proof of the effective service of my friend on this occasion, he was rewarded and honoured by the King of Saxony with the Cross of Civil Merit; whilst the King of Prussia, and several of the reigning Dukes of Germany, presented him with handsome testimonials in token of his valuable services.

As Cicerone to Mr. Ackermann's Gallery, my friend, William Henry Pyne, was engaged, and in that capacity was respectably and profitably employed, both for himself and for his worthy master. The former had published, and progressively produced numerous works, both graphic and literary, in all of which, from partialities and experience, Pyne became eminently useful. Hence the artist and the printseller worked in harmony and unison for some years, and jointly completed several publications on the fine arts, topography, and poetry. Besides several lessons, elementary books and prints, for the instruction of young artists, they brought forward a large and expensive work, entitled "The Microcosm of London," 3 vols. royal 4to. with 120 illustrative prints. To Mr. Ackermann we are indebted for the introduction into England, and for effecting many improvements in the new art, of Lithography, by translating and giving publicity to Senefelder's Treatise on the subject; a work that excited much curiosity, speculation, and experiments among the artists. He also imported stones for that novel process, and by adapting presses and paper, and by the employment of competent artists to make drawings, progressively, but slowly, advanced lithography to distinction. The following lines were written by Mr. Combe on the first lithograph stone which Mr. Ackermann printed, when he had prepared everything for working:

"I have been told of one
Who, being ask'd for bread,
In its stead
Return'd a Stone:

"But here we manage better;
The Stone, we ask
To do its task,
And it returns us every letter.
"Wm. Combe, January 23, 1817."

He was the first publisher of a class of books, called "Annuals," by his "Forget-me-Not," which became exceedingly popular, and was a source of employ to numerous artists, authors, and different tradesmen. The "Forget-me-Not" was edited, from its commencement in 1823, to its last volume in 1834, by F. Shoberl, one of the most industrious, persevering, and honourable of the literary fraternity, who has been solely, or mostly, dependant on his profession for a livelihood. Watt, in "Bibliotheca Britannica," has given a long list of his publications, in translations from the French and German, original and compilations, from 1800 to 1814, since which year he has written a further and longer list of works: amongst others I perceive that his name is attached to the histories of the counties of Suffolk, Surrey, and Sussex, forming one of the volumes of "The Beauties of England."

A history of this literary family—"the Annuals"—would embrace much curious anecdote, biography, and exposition of art and artists; of professional and amateur authors; of trade, manufactures, and commerce; of fashion, fame, and frivolity; and last, though not the least, the fluctuation and caprices of taste and ton. The "Annuals," which were so popular and profitable to a Heath, and a Fisher, twenty years ago, are now superseded, and a totally different and new species has been introduced by Messrs. Longman and Co. and by Virtue; in which topography, history, travels, and substantial literature are the basis.

His large and handsome volumes, with illustrations, of Westminster Abbey, of Cambridge, Oxford, and of Public Schools, were amongst the most beautiful topographical works of their class, in paper, typography, and embellishments. The writing, though anonymous, was by William

Combe, one of the most extraordinary men of his age, and who ranks amongst the most prolific of authors.

Though I was never on intimate terms with this talented and eccentric person, I knew him personally by meeting him often at the houses of my friends, the Ackermanns, and James Lonsdale, portrait-painter of Berners Street. Combe was of good family connection, had received a classical education at Eton and Oxford, and very early came into the possession of a large fortune, in ready money. To dash at once into high life, and enact the fashionable gentleman, he (according to his own narration) took a large mansion at "the West End" of London, furnished and filled it with gorgeous articles, and also hired servants, bought carriages, &c., and successively assembled around him a crowd of sycophants and the "beau-monde." This comedy, or rather farce, lasted only for a short time, and it is said that from the commencement to the drop-scene of the ridiculous drama, was not more than one year. Though he fancied this gave him an insight into high life, it is quite evident that the company thus assembled, and thus held together, could only be of a class which ought to rank below the low—gamblers, swindlers, tricksters, imposters, &c. The consequence was ruin—complete, disgraceful ruin, and Combe fled from his creditors and from society. We next hear of him as a common soldier, and recognized at a public-house with a volume of Greek poetry in his hand. He was relieved from this degrading situation, and henceforward, for a long period, the annals of his life have been pretty fully detailed. The walls of the King's Bench Prison, and "the Rules" of that famed establishment, were the limits and sphere of his locomotion; and from his conduct, manners, and general deportment in society, they do not appear to have proved causes of much punishment or lamentation. Horace Smith, in the Memoirs of his witty and much-caressed brother, James, says, that Colonel Greville, with several of his friends, established a Pic-nic club for theatrical amusements, &c., and published a newspaper to vindicate their association from severe strictures that appeared in the daily papers against them. Our imprisoned hero was appointed the paid editor, and, to suit his peculiarity of situation, the weekly meetings of the writers of articles were held after dark. Horace Smith, who knew Combe, justly remarks, that "a faithful biography of this singular character might justly be entitled a romance of real life; so strange were the adventures and the freaks of fortune of which he had been a participator and a victim. A ready writer of all-work for the booksellers, he passed all the latter portion of his time within 'the Rules,' to which suburban retreat the present writer was occasionally invited, and never left him without admiring his various acquirements, and the philosophical equanimity with which he endured his reverses." Mr. Smith further asserts, that if there was a lack of matter occasionally to fill up the columns of their paper, "Combe would sit down in the publisher's back room and extemporize a letter from Sterne at Coxwold, a forgery so well executed that it never excited suspicion." I cannot but regret that my witty friend had not favoured us with more anecdotes of, and remarks on, the character and literary talents of Combe; but I can easily excuse him when I reflect on the superabundance of material which his memory and his memoranda must have afforded for the two amusing volumes he had planned of his brother's memorable "sayings and doings." Were I disposed to dwell on the character of Combe, I could extend the present description to several pages. He was born in 1741, and died in June 1814. Subsequent to his death, a small volume was published, entitled "Letters to Marianne," said to have been written by him after the age of seventy to a young girl, and, according to the "Literary Gazette," are trivial, silly, puerile. However eventful and amusing may be the adventures and vicissitudes of such a man as Combe, if narrated by a Dickens, a Thackeray, or a Douglas Jerrold, I must resign the task to such vivid writers, or their followers, and merely refer to the "Gentleman's Magazine," for May 1852, for a communication from my friend, Mr. R. Cole, who has a large collection of Autograph Letters and Manuscripts, amongst which is a detailed list of the literary works of, and numerous letters from and to Combe.

The engravings of Westminster Abbey, of Cambridge, Oxford, and of the Public Schools were in aquatint, and coloured in imitation of the original drawings, by Mackenzie, Pugin, W. Westall, F. Nash, W. Turner, and others: many of them represent interior views of the principal public buildings. There are also prints of full-length portraits from drawings by T. Uwins, and etchings by J. Agar, representing the official costume of all the different orders of Officers of the Universities. Mr. Ackermann also brought out a Poetical Magazine, which became the parent of a race of novel publications of unprecedented notoriety. These were a sort of hybrid twins of poetry and art, in the illustrated, or rhyming, rambling, ricketty, and ridiculous poems, "Dr. Syntax's Tour in Search of the Picturesque." The work not only passed through several editions, of three Tours, but extended to three volumes; and within the last few years they have been again brought before the public at reduced prices by Mr. H. G. Bohn. "Dr. Syntax" was a lucky and large prize in the lottery of publication, and was also a novelty in origin and writing. Instead of the composition and designs for the illustrations growing out of, and serving to ornament and give tangible forms, figures, colours, effects, &c., to the language and imaginings of the poet, or other writer; the artist, in the work referred to, preceded the author by making a series of drawings; in each of which he exhibited his hero in a succession of places, and in various associations, calculated to exemplify his hobby-horsical search for the picturesque. Some of these drawings, by the versatile and ingenious artist, Rowlandson, were shown at a dinner-party, at John Bannister's, in Gower Street, when it was agreed they should be recommended to Ackermann for publication. That gentleman readily purchased, and handed them by two or three at a time to Combe, when the latter was in the King's Bench. He fitted them with rhymes, and they made their first appearance in the magazine alluded to. Exciting much popularity, the publisher reproduced them in separate volumes, and found demand keep pace with his supply. Hence "Syntax" was succeeded by "The Dance of Life," "The Dance of Death," "Johnny Quæ Genus," and "Tom Raw the Griffin," all of the same class and character, and ultimately extending to two hundred and ninety-five prints, with annotatory poetical letter-press.

Without adverting further, in this place, to the periodical press and publishers, generally, I cannot forbear to notice two weekly journals which had their birth in this locality, and which have proved themselves resolute and powerful advocates of moral, political, and literary reforms: viz., "The Examiner," and the "Literary Gazette." The former was projected and undertaken by two enthusiastic young men, almost boys, John and Leigh Hunt, who thought patriotism and literature were the only thing worth living for; and believing themselves not only slighted, but oppressed by the rulers of the land, thought that it would be glorious, either to obtain emancipation, or suffer martyrdom in the attempt. They paid dearly for their rashness and courage, as may be seen fully set forth, with honest candour and truthfulness, by the latter, in his Auto-Biography, in 3 vols., published in 1850, to which work I can refer the reader, with an assurance that he will find much amusing as well as eloquent and exciting commentary on the popular events and persons of the half-century after the year 1800.

Amongst the literary persons of the present century, that voluminous author ranks in the first class. From boyhood (for he was a precocious poet), up to the present time (1853), his whole time and mental energies appear to have been employed in literature; and the amount, variety, and merits of his numerous published writings are at once manifestations of industry, enthusiasm, zeal, an ardent love of liberty, and of the better productions of genius and talent. His first volume, intituled "Juvenilia," was a series of poems written between the ages of twelve and sixteen. It appeared in the year 1801, when, I believe, he was in "The Blue-Coat School," and a contemporary with the two brilliant intellectual planets in the hemisphere of talent, Coleridge and Lamb. The times when his first volume made its public appearance, when its author sought the approval of critics and patrons, were rife with political excitement and contention. Party spirit was violent and rancorous; and every person who possessed warm feelings and thinking powers became imperceptibly a jacobin, or an anti-jacobin: i. e., a Reformer, or a Tory, opposed to all changes. Mr. Leigh Hunt and his brother John avowed themselves of the former class, and started their "Examiner," as a medium to promulgate their sentiments, and oppose both the opinions and principles of the other party.

The consequence was, State prosecutions and consequent heavy fines, as well as cruel imprisonment. Unintimidated and unflinching, they continued to publish the "Examiner," and also continued to occupy its weekly columns with severe and caustic writings on the malpractices of ministers, and on the vices and follies of those princes, nobles, and commoners, who lived and luxuriated on the revenues of the State.

One department of their paper was devoted to the "Fine Arts," the criticisms and comments on which were mostly written by Robert Hunt, brother of the two partners. Related to Benjamin West, the President of the Royal Academy, and having been educated as an artist, this gentleman rendered his critical articles popular and influential. He wrote two or three Essays for me, which appeared in "The Fine Arts of the English School;" and also produced others for different publications.

"The Literary Gazette," which made its first appearance on the 25th of January, 1817, has proved eminently serviceable in promoting the national literature, as well as its fine arts. It was at first the property of Mr. Colburn, an active and enterprising publisher, who possessed "The New Monthly Magazine," and other works of popularity, and who eagerly availed himself of every channel to attract the notice, and excite the curiosity, of readers. A new medium was found in this Gazette, which not merely professed to advocate, but to bring forward the better specimens of literature, and scout and expose its quackery. It is generally admitted that it was almost constantly kind, generous, and complimentary to young aspirants for fame—in authorship, art, and the drama. I cannot, however, forget, or palliate the severity it manifested towards a youthful Poet of real genius and equal modesty, who ventured to launch a small volume on the "sea of troubles," and which was assailed by the "Literary Gazette" in unqualified terms of reprobation. The principal poem was "Richmond Hill," a site calculated to arouse the most intense admiration in every lover of the fine and beautiful scenery of nature. In his verses on this fascinating prospect, I may safely assert that Charles Ellis evinced ardent feelings as well as genuine sympathies for the beauties of the scene, and also genuine, if not the highest, poetical powers to depict them.

The new periodical ultimately proved a large prize in the lottery of book-speculation, as it progressively rose high in the thermometer of fashion and fame. Its progress and fluctuating annals would afford abundance of interest to the general reader, were they fully and faithfully narrated. Mr. William Jerdan, who tells us in his Auto-Biography that he was its "sole editor and part-proprietor, from its commencement to August 14, 1841," has narrated many particulars of its contents, contributors, proprietors, and changes. To that work I must refer my reader, as well as for an account of the literary career and worldly vicissitudes of an old friend, with whom I have continued in occasional correspondence and personal intercourse for nearly forty years: I cannot, however, help deeply regretting to read his account of the profession of authorship; it being so much at variance with my own experience and opinions. These I have partly explained in the "The Rights of Literature," in "The Authorship of the Letters of Junius Elucidated," and in other parts of my numerous publications. On referring to past volumes of the "Literary Gazette," I always find them replete with valuable and interesting information on the contemporary literature, the fine arts, science, and the drama; also on the manners and customs of the constantly changing times from 1817 to 1850. The recent numbers of this weekly periodical show it to be conducted by an editor of science, candour, and literary talents.

The Strand has long been known as the place of congress of certain learned and eminent national societies, whose "Transactions" have travelled to, and been located and studied in, all the civilized cities of the globe. Those of the Royal, the Antiquaries, and the Astronomical, have free quarters within the government edifice of Somerset House; whilst the Society of Arts, in a noble mansion of its own, has taken root and prospered, in John Street, close to the Strand. The history of each and all of these societies is replete with interesting matter, not merely for the archæologist and scientific, but for the historian of man, in developing the progress of his intellectual qualifications. Mr. Weld has given to the public a well-digested history of that of the Royal, and it is hoped that other authors will shortly produce similar publications on their respective societies.

No. 32 in the Strand was a large print-shop, belonging to Mr. Richardson, whose extensive collection was noted for portraits, topographical and antiquarian prints, and for public sales of that class of property. In February and March, 1800, he sold an amazing collection of British portraits, which continued for thirty-one days, and which appears to have been accumulating for forty years. He was also employed on many other similar occasions to dispose of graphic works. During the winter he frequently had sales in the evening, which I often attended, and as often puchased "lots." Here I met several gentlemen, with whom I became intimate, from congeniality of attachments. Amongst these were Mr. Alexander, of the British Museum, Mr. Baker, of St. Paul's Churchyard, Mr. R. Holford, Mr. Bentham, Mr. Bindley, Dr. Gossett, Mr. Molteno, and several others, whose hoards have since been again brought to the hammer, and distributed to amuse other illustrators. Richardson published several portraits, fac-similes of scarce prints, and also three different-sized prints of the "Felton Shakspeare," as it is usually named. At his rooms were sold by auction the famed collections of Musgrave and of Tighe.

In the Strand were the shops of Mr. Faden, Mr. Cary, and Mr. Smith, who entirely devoted themselves to Geography, by publishing Maps, Charts, Globes, &c. I often visited them to obtain and communicate information. The most important topographical surveys were published by Mr. Faden, but they were too expensive for my pocket. This gentleman has been succeeded by James Wyld, Esq., M. P., who has brought into the business more energy and enterprise than his predecessor, and has consequently produced great changes and improvements in his published works. As a feature of the times in which we live, we find that Mr. Wyld is a member of the Legislature, and a bold competitor with the daring and unparalleled Crystal Palace of 1851, by designing and constructing a building, with an exhibition to display the geographical surface of the terrestrial Globe. The invention and the execution are honourable to his name and country; and it is hoped that it will reward his enterprise.

I always travelled with the best small map I could obtain, and marked in such alterations and corrections as I met with. These were handed over to the publishers, and consequently inserted in new impressions of their respective plates. The Trigonometrical and the Ordnance Surveys were not published when I walked round Wales, into Cornwall, and through some other districts. These truly important national works are now produced, and, being sold at very low prices, are of incalculable value to modern antiquaries and topographers.

Near the western end of the Strand, on the North side, was the house of a Mr. Baxter, having in the rear a large Room, which he let out for private theatricals, for debates, and for readings and music. His wife possessed a fine soprano voice, played well on the piano-forte, and occasionally performed on the stage. At this place I became acquainted with George Saville Carey, who published a small volume called "Balnea, or Sketches of Watering-places," 1799, which, I believe, was the first work that gave a general account of those famed places of fashionable resort; and it would be interesting to show the extent, population, &c., of Bath, Brighton, Leamington, Margate, and Buxton, as they were when that volume was published, and as they now are. Carey wrote a volume on "Mimicry," and was famed for his Imitations of Garrick, Henderson, Kemble, Mrs. Siddons, and others. I have a vivid recollection of the mellow, flexible voice, and expressive intonations of Garrick, as well as the dull, phlegmatic, monotonous tones of Kemble, as Carey displayed them: one was mellifluous to the ear, the other grating and discordant, though not quite so bad as Coleman describes it

dies, amongst whom were the Duke of Sussex, Mr. Wilberforce, and other personages of rank. Before he quitted London, he published an octavo volume, with his portrait engraved by Charles Turner. Its title is: "By Authority. Haytian Papers: A Collection of the very Interesting Proclamations, and other Official Documents; together with some Account of the Rise, Progress, and Present State of the Kingdom of Hayti. With a Preface by Prince Sanders, Esq., Agent for the Haytian Government. London: printed for W. Reed, 17, Fleet Street." 8vo. 1816. This volume is a curiosity. I never heard what became of its editor, after he left London; but I learnt that several other persons, as well as myself, had been imposed on by him.

Connected with the Strand are reminiscences of the Lyceum Theatre, with my public appearance on its stage, and in the stage-box; of Robert Ker Porter's exhibition of Seringapatam and other pictures; of the wonderful mimicry, ventriloquism, and transformations of Monsieur Alexandre, the rival of Mathews; of Phillipstall's Phantasmagoria; and also of the "Sans Pareil Theatre," as it was called in 1806, when Mr. Scott, a colour-maker, built and fitted it up for his daughter, who made her first public appearance there, and gained much applause for songs and recitations. This lady's performances, united with mechanical and optical illusions, gave character to the house, and made the fortune of its proprietor. "Tom and Jerry," by Pierce Egan, afterwards attracted immense crowds, when the name of "Little Adelphi." was given to the theatre. In 1825 Terry and Yates became lessees, but lost money. Charles Mathews joined the latter, and continued to give his popular and profitable "At Home" here for three successive years. It was at this house I first became acquainted with that extraordinary actor, mimic, and man, and continued to meet him frequently afterwards. He was born in 1776, at No. 18 in the Strand, and died in 1835, after a long career of theatrical adventure, vicissitude, and fame. Among the numerous volumes of biography and auto-biography of the heroes and heroines of the sock and buskin, there is not one surpassing in variety, wit, and amusement, that of the eccentric and much-admired Charles Mathews. It is written jointly by the player and his widow, and extends to four volumes. A few pages only of the first are by the pen of the former, and the remainder is admirably executed by the latter.

At No. 145, Strand, were the book-shop and auction-rooms of Messrs. Leigh and Sotheby, at the beginning of the present century, in which many choice and costly books were transferred from one collector to another. Mr. Leigh was established as an auctioneer in King Street, Covent Garden, in 1744; and from that time to the present the Catalogues, with prices and purchasers' names, are preserved by the present respectable firm in Wellington Street.

After the decease of the first gentleman, the second continued the business for some years in the same street, and disposed of many celebrated libraries. He has been succeeded by his worthy Son, who inherits many of the good points of his much-respected parent, and equally respected partner, retaining the names of both. Since the retirement of Mr. Evans, of Pall Mall, Mr. Samuel Leigh Sotheby has been most extensively occupied in selling distinguished libraries, and, I believe, with credit to himself and advantage to his employers. On comparing one of his recent catalogues, for Samuel Prout, with another printed for his godfather and father, in 1806, of nine days' sale of the library of one of my earliest literary friends, the Rev. Jonathan Boucher, the contrast is remarkable. The last exhibits bad type, bad ink, bad paper, and heedless editorship; whilst the former is the reverse in all these qualities: yet the Boucher Catalogue is charged 3s. 6d., and that of Prout's Collection was given away. Mr. Sotheby's partner (John Wilkinson) conducts the selling department with as much zeal and promptitude as the former manifests in arrangement, catalogueing, and in other parts of the business. Their rooms are now in Wellington Street.

In alluding to the Auction-rooms of the western part of London, it would seem negligent or invidious were I to omit two which have been justly eminent in credit and respectability for many years in the early part of the present century: those of Robert H. Evans, No. 93, Pall Mall, and James Christie, first in Pall Mall, and afterwards in King Street, St. James's. Brief notices of the numerous and various sales of books, MSS. and prints which have been distributed over the world by the first auctioneer, would extend to a large volume, and might be made particularly interesting to the lovers of literature. It would embrace accounts of a vast variety of valuable and important books, whose histories involve not merely their own intrinsic merits and peculiarities, but the fluctuations of prices and caprices of purchasers. Some have been highly prized and hoarded for their scarcity, (a lamentable criterion, as many of these

the beginning of the present century, in which many choice and costly books were transferred from one collector to another. Mr. Leigh was established as an auctioneer in King Street, Covent Garden, in 1744; and from that time to the present the Catalogues, with prices and purchasers' names, are preserved by the present respectable firm in Wellington Street.

After the decease of the first gentleman, the second continued the business for some years in the same street, and disposed of many celebrated libraries. He has been succeeded by his worthy Son, who inherits many of the good points of his much-respected parent, and equally respected partner, retaining the names of both. Since the retirement of Mr. Evans, of Pall Mall, Mr. Samuel Leigh Sotheby has been most extensively occupied in selling distinguished libraries, and, I believe, with credit to himself and advantage to his employers. On comparing one of his recent catalogues, for Samuel Prout, with another printed for his godfather and father, in 1806, of nine days' sale of the library of one of my earliest literary friends, the Rev. Jonathan Boucher, the contrast is remarkable. The last exhibits bad type, bad ink, bad paper, and heedless editorship; whilst the former is the reverse in all these qualities: yet the Boucher Catalogue is charged 3s. 6d., and that of Prout's Collection was given away. Mr. Sotheby's partner (John Wilkinson) conducts the selling department with as much zeal and promptitude as the former manifests in arrangement, catalogueing, and in other parts of the business. Their rooms are now in Wellington Street.

In alluding to the Auction-rooms of the western part of London, it would seem negligent or invidious were I to omit two which have been justly eminent in credit and respectability for many years in the early part of the present century: those of Robert H. Evans, No. 93, Pall Mall, and James Christie, first in Pall Mall, and afterwards in King Street, St. James's. Brief notices of the numerous and various sales of books, MSS. and prints which have been distributed over the world by the first auctioneer, would extend to a large volume, and might be made particularly interesting to the lovers of literature. It would embrace accounts of a vast variety of valuable and important books, whose histories involve not merely their own intrinsic merits and peculiarities, but the fluctuations of prices and caprices of purchasers. Some have been highly prized and hoarded for their scarcity, (a lamentable criterion, as many of these "extremely rare" articles are worthless); others for being a trifle larger in the margin than another copy which has been pronounced the tallest; whilst a third quality is the possession of some cancelled leaf or print, which was originally deemed useless, or objectionable. I have often seen the large sale-room crowded by real lovers of literature, by collectors, by bibliographers, and by bibliomaniacs, and witnessed the enormous prices given for books, both of intrinsic beauty and merit, and of capricious worth. The Roxburgh, the Sykes, the Spencer, the Hibbert, the Dent, the Hoare, and the Broadley libraries were noted for their extent, value, scarcity, and for other peculiarities: some of these have been sold and resold by auction since their first appearance in a sale-room. Dibdin's "Library Companion," his "Bibliomania," and his "Reminiscences," contain much curious information on the subjects here referred to: and I must not omit to notice my respected friend Mr. Clarke's "Repertorium Bibliographicum," a large royal octavo volume of 1819, which contains much valuable and curious information on celebrated British libraries, and their choicest book-treasures.

Mr. Christie's Sale-rooms, in Pall Mall and in King Street, have been noted for more than half a century, as well for the high respectability and qualifications of the auctioneers, as for the vast amount and nature of the property they have exhibited. I have known three generations of the family, and had reason to esteem each and all. Though I saw but little of the first, who was famed for his bland and engaging manners and voice, as well as for his florid, spontaneous addresses, or panegyrics, yet I never see the exquisite portrait of him, in the counting-house of King Street, without emotions of admiration of the artist, and the auctioneer. On referring to a catalogue of "a most capital and precious assemblage of pictures" by Mr. Christie, Sen., whose "Great Room" was in Pall Mall, June 13th, 1807, I see a flourishing, and rather a Robins-like account of a small collection of only 44 pictures, each of which is highly eulogised. One of them, by Rembrandt, is described as "the finest picture, without exception, ever painted by that master." The Catalogue is marked 2s. 6d. George H. Christie succeeded his parent in 1831, in the same premises, and in the same career of high character, and in costly sales of works of art and vertu. In the same year Peter Coxe, author of "The Social Day," a poem, sold a small gallery of "original paintings, the property of Mr. Andrew Wilson," the Catalogue of which, marked 2s. 6d., contains a highly coloured advertisement, with comments on each "painting," also praised. He was brother of Archdeacon Coxe, and a popular auctioneer for some years. Amongst other sales was one of the Bowood collection of pictures, out of which I purchased three, by Sir Joshua Reynolds, Romney, and Wright, of Derby. The first and second were transferred to the Marquis of Stafford, and the third, half-length of the Marquis of Granby, to a gentleman of Devonshire.

With the late James Christie I was familiarly acquainted, in his public and private characteristics; and though I occasionally lamented to see him in his auction-rostrum, surrounded by unshaven and rude brokers, and sometimes subjected to the cant language of such "gents," I also saw him in the company of nobles of the land, and commoners of equally noble character. With the latter, my amiable friend seemed "at home," and addressed them in language and manners which could not fail to propitiate their confidence and respect. More than once I have attended his sales, for the purpose of seeing certain fine pictures, and also to bid for some on account of friends. The celebrated series of Hogarth's "Election" I bought for Sir John Soane, at what was thought to be a large sum. The lot excited competition, and the auctioneer made occasional pauses and a few opposite and judicious remarks between the biddings. On knocking it down, he pronounced as neat and pointed an address to the successful candidate as ever was heard at any electioneering contest in the united kingdom. Mr. Christie, Sen., died in 1805; and James Christie, his Son, in 1831, aged 57.

In King Street, Covent Garden, were the Auction-rooms of King and Lochee, chiefly devoted to books, in which I was first tempted to compete for a few topographical articles in 1800. It was the library of Philip Luckombe, who had published a small "History of Printing," in 1771; "A Tour in Ireland, 1783;" and "England's Gazetteer," in 1790, in 3 volumes, 12mo.; also some other works; whence it appears that he had been connected with the press. His library, though small, contained Camden's Britannia, interleaved and illustrated; his own "Gazetteer," interleaved, with MS. Notes; also other topographical books. There being but little competition, I laid out about £20, and carried away a hackney coach load of literary materials for future reference and application.

At the same rooms, the Rev. Dr. Richard Farmer's large library had been sold in 1798; extending over thirty-six days.

My (Britton) earliest aspirations, after engaging to write on Topography, were to cultivate the acquaintance of those persons, who either sold or collected books, prints, or other articles in that class of literature; and that I progressively and ultimately became familiar with most of the bibliopolists, print-sellers, and auction-rooms in the metropolis. My limited funds, however, precluded me from purchasing to a great extent; but I may safely aver that, from the year 1800 to 1850, there was not one Olympic cycle passed without an increase of my library, in books, prints, and drawings. As already remarked, my fit of Bibliomania was first caught at the sale of the library of Philip Luckombe, when I obtained the "Britannia," with printed, manuscript, and graphic accompaniments.

Thenceforward the disease increased in strength, and I continued to frequent nearly all the book sales of London, in which topography and antiquities constituted any distinguished portion. On these occasions, I not only became acquainted with eminent collectors, but also obtained some knowledge of the relative merits and value of books. Unlike many of my associates at these competing marts, I never sought to possess works which were valued and purchased merely from rarity, or dimensions of margin. Fine paper and good prints I coveted, and sometimes bought. Under these influences, and of warm temperament, it is not surprising that my own collection increased to an unwieldly and inconvenient extent. My rooms, boxes, closets, &c., were crowded, whilst the purse collapsed, and I deemed it prudent to commission Mr. Southgate to sell some of the books at his rooms. In June, 1832, I sent enough to make up six days' sale; and subsequently, at different times, have sold a sufficient number to occupy ten more days. Every sale, however, furnished cause of mortification and sorrow; for books, drawings, prints, and objects of vertu, were sold at very low prices.

The following Address was written and printed by Mr. Britton in June, 1832, to accompany Catalogues sent to particular persons; and is reprinted, in this place, as expressive of the feelings and opinions he then experienced and entertained on such a subject.

BOOKS: READING, STUDY.

A man who has been actively engaged for forty years in collecting, and in using Books,—who during that space of time has been economical in all his other expences for the purpose of indulging this "hobby," and who has also been much occupied in the pleasure of writing, and penalties of publishing, will be likely to find the said hobby grow rather too large for his stable, and demand more than common care and labour in "looking after." Though thus overgrown and incommodious, I can truly re-echo the sentiment of Cumberland, who in his "Memoirs" asserts, that his "books and pen have been his never-failing comforters and friends."

From these, and all other earthly ties, a time of parting must arrive; and Books will have failed in one of their important duties, or qualities, if they have not inculcated the lesson of submitting to inevitable events, without unavailing murmur. Philosophy has many pretty maxims, but it has not one among the number to render sensibility insensible. It certainly teaches us "to bear the ills we have," and guard against, or ward off others, which may assail us. Dr. Kitchener instructed "every man to make his own Will"—and he might have taught him, also, to be his own Executor. This would tend to shorten lawyers' bills, and lengthen legacies; would benefit widows and orphans, and abridge posthumous taxation. If there were no other reasons for a man's looking beyond the grave, than a desire of saving litigation, and mulcts to the tax office, these were sufficient; but how often and how effectually can he apply his superfluous property—if he has any—towards the end of his life, if he has resolution and good feelings, to bequeath it to deserving relatives and friends.

Let us hear what Petrarch said of Books, about five hundred years ago, when there were neither Magazines nor Reviews, and when printing and engraving were alike unknown, and let us endeavour to appreciate and profit by his just and philosophical remarks.

"Some people consider the pleasures of the world as their supreme good, and not to be renounced. But I have friends of a very different description (my Books), whose society is far more agreeable to me: they are of all countries, and of all ages; they are distinguished in war, in politics, and in the sciences. It is very easy to see them; they are always at my service. I call for their company, or send them away, whenever I please: they are never troublesome, and immediately answer all my questions. Some relate the events of ages past, others reveal the secrets of nature; these teach me how to live in comfort, those how to die in quiet. In return for all these services, they only require a chamber of me in one corner of my mansion, where they may repose in peace."

If, however, instead of one corner of his mansion, Petrarch had found every room and every closet of his house filled with these dear friends, he might have experienced some inconvenience from their company, and been induced, like myself and many others, to turn some of them out of doors, for the purpose of seeing and enjoying the selected few.

A short account of the rise and progress of the Library, of which a part is now to be disposed of, will "point a moral," if not "adorn a tale." In boyhood I attended the sale of a country 'squire's furniture, &c., and bought a lot of nine books for 1s. One of them was "Robinson Crusoe," which I read with avidity, and longed to be cast on a desert island, with a "Man Friday." This library travelled with me to London, and occupied—with Bailey's Dictionary, a few magazines, some anatomical and medical books, &c.—a small deal box, during six years of miserable apprenticeship, the greater part of which was spent in a murky, damp, and dirty cellar. Sanguine in hopes, and ardently looking forward to emancipation from a sad state of legal slavery, my health gave way, and I became weak, emaciated, and desponding. But for the "little knowledge" obtained even from my small library, I should have sunk into an early grave; from books I acquired some knowledge of my own constitution, frame of body, and the latent disease which exhibited evident symptoms of consumption. Thus, I attribute prolongation of life to reading. At the end of apprenticeship my boy-library contained twenty-five volumes, and my purse five guineas. For the ensuing ten years my stock increased but very slowly; a small nest of shelves held the whole. Commencing with Mr. Brayley the "Beauties of England," in 1800, it became necessary to have nearly every printed book relating to the counties described; but as these were expensive, they were retained only as long as wanted, and then sold to purchase others. This class of reading and writing excited a desire to possess a library, and every new year not only increased the desire, but also augmented the collection.

In Tavistock Place it occupied three sides of a small room nine feet square, and I then thought myself truly rich and happy. Infected with the "Bibliomania," which raged for some time in London, I was impelled to attend the sale rooms of King and Lochee—Richardson—Leigh and Sotheby—Evans, and other famed "contagionists"—

where I continued to purchase, as if "increase of appetite grew with what it fed on." Many "curious, choice, and rare articles" have thus come into my possession, which I have seen pass through the hands of three or four "famous" collectors. Here the retrospect is painful, and melancholy; for it brings before imagination the Names, Tales, and varied Characters of the indefatigable and zealous Strutt—the eccentric and enthusiastic Carter—the magnificent Lansdowne—the amiable and learned Boucher—the plodding and laborious Reed—the talented but splenetic Steevens and Ritson—the universally esteemed Alexander—the ostentatious Dent—the historical Coxe, cum multis aliis.

www.ingramcontent.com/pod-product-compliance
Lightning Source LLC
Chambersburg PA
CBHW022116160426
43197CB00009B/1044